THE RAMBLERS' ASSOCIATION

DEVON WALKS WITH A POINT

THE RAMBLERS' ASSOCIATION

DEVON WALKS WITH A POINT

Janice Anderson

W. Foulsham & Co. Ltd.
London · New York · Toronto · Cape Town · Sydney

The Ramblers' Association
1-5 Wandsworth Road,
London SW8 2LJ

W. Foulsham & Company Limited
Yeovil Road, Slough, Berkshire, SL1 4JH

The author wishes to thank Will Adams for his great help in checking the details of several walks in this book.

ISBN 0-572-01354-X

Please note:
Although every effort has been made to ensure that the details given in this book are accurate, the author, the publishers and the Ramblers' Association cannot accept responsibility for any changes or alterations to the information since the research was carried out. Where public rights of way are concerned any obstacle or hindrance should be reported to the Ramblers' Association (see page 9).

Printed in Great Britain
at St. Edmundsbury Press, Bury St. Edmunds.

Cover Photo: Simon Watts
Arlington Court (Walk 9)
Black and white photographs by Edmund Swinglehurst

INFORMATION ABOUT THE RAMBLERS' ASSOCIATION

The Ramblers' Association is a registered charity with three main aims.

- to protect footpaths and other rights of way and increase access to open country.
- to defend outstanding landscapes.
- to encourage people to walk in the countryside.

It carries out these aims at a national level, through the employment of staff to run national campaigns, lobby MPs, etc. and generally organise the work of the Association, and at a local level through the activities of the voluntary workers in its Areas and Groups, who tackle problems on paths, both by reporting them to highway authorities and by carrying out practical work, such as stile building and waymaking. The Areas and Groups also have programmes of rambles and other events.

Since it was formed in 1935 the RA has grown steadily, and in 1985 membership topped 50,000 for the first time. The RA's branch structure has also developed, in particular through the formation of local Groups within Areas.

The threats to the countryside and its paths are growing, and so are our needs. You can help simply by becoming a member. There are plenty of opportunities for joining in the practical footpath and amenity work carried out by your local RA Group.

As a member you will be able to take advantage of the

following benefits.

■ A **local group** to walk with (but go on your own if you prefer); most groups run social events too. ■ Free annual **Bed and Breakfast Guide** with more than 2,000 addresses where walkers are welcome. ■ **Rucksack**, the RA's own magazine, plus your own area news, four times a year. ■ Use of our 1:50,000 Ordnance Survey **map library**. ■ **Discounts** in more than 100 outdoor equipment shops. ■ **Special offers on publications**; a discount subscription to **The Great Outdoors** magazine. ■ Access to our national service of **expert advice and information**.

PROTECTING THE FOOTPATH HERITAGE

INTRODUCTION

The information given below is about the law relating to public rights of way in England and Wales.

Public paths are highways in law. They have the same legal protection in principle as metalled carriageways, the difference being that paths are dedicated to use by limited classes of traffic, i.e. walkers on footpaths; and walkers, riders and cyclists on bridleways.

An old legal maxim says that once a highway always a highway. This means that a public path can only be closed by statutory procedure. It does not cease to be a right of way simply because it is unused or little used.

HOW YOU CAN HELP

Paths are part of our heritage and need our protection. Every time you walk along a path you help to keep it open. By varying routes to include little known paths and by reporting any difficulties you meet you can make every step count in the struggle to preserve our country walks.

Reporting difficulties. Write to the appropriate local authority (see below) and tell the RA. Give location (six figure grid reference) and nature of problem, path number and name of owner or tenant (if known). RA national office will supply you with obstruction report forms ready for use.

Obstructions. An obstruction is anything which hinders your free passage along the path, e.g. a barbed wire fence where there should be a gap or stile. County councils have a statutory duty to keep public paths open for public use and enjoyment.

Ploughing. It is illegal to plough a path along a field boundary. The farmer is required to leave room between the hedge or fence and the cultivated area for the path. Paths going across fields may be ploughed, provided that the farmer restores the path within two weeks of ploughing. Report infringements to county or district councils.

Bridges and overgrowth. A missing bridge or overgrowth on the surface of the path are within the highway authority's maintenance responsibilities. The highway authorities are the county councils but some district councils have taken over maintenance from the counties. Overgrowth from the sides of the path should be dealt with by the owner or tenant of the land. The highway authority has power to act if he does not.

Misleading notices, i.e. any signs which by false or misleading information may deter people from using a public path, are an offence on paths shown on the definitive map. Report to highway authority.

Bulls. No bull over the age of ten months is allowed to be at large on its own in a field crossed by a public path, and no bull of a recognised dairy breed (Ayrshire, British Friesian, British Holstein, Dairy Shorthorn, Guernsey, Jersey and Kerry) is allowed in such a field under any circumstances. It is not a specific offence for beef and cross breed bulls to be at large in fields crossed by public paths if they are accompanied by cows or heifers, but if the bull endangers public safety an offence may be committed under section 3 of the Health and Safety at Work Act 1974. Report any problems to the police.

PRACTICAL WORK

Increasingly, branches of the RA and local footpath and amenity societies are undertaking practical work to improve the condition of the paths.

This takes two main forms: path clearance and waymarking. Waymarking is carried out by painting arrows at points along the path where the route is unclear.

FURTHER READING

A brief exposition of the law in England and Wales is contained in a leaflet published by the RA, *Right of Way*. The RA also publishes, in conjunction with the Open Spaces Society, *Rights of Way: a Guide to Law and Practice*, a comprehensive 368-page book which includes the text of the relevant legislation. The RA also sells *Footpaths: a practical handbook* published by the British Trust for Conservation Volunteers, which is a most comprehensive guide to practical work.

CONTENTS

	Route and direction of walk	PH	Public house
A385	A Road		Settlement
B3212	B Road		Building
	All other roads and tracks		Church
	Footpath		Bridge
	Railway		Weir
	Canal		Quarry
P	Parking		Triangulation pillar
	Viewpoint		Woodland
	Golf course		Lake
			Tumulus
			Cairn

The maps

The sketch maps in this book are meant to be used in conjunction with the Ordnance Survey map mentioned at the beginning of each walk. Symbols on the maps have been simplified and are meant to give rough guidance to the location of symbols on the Ordnance Survey map.

LOCATION OF WALKS

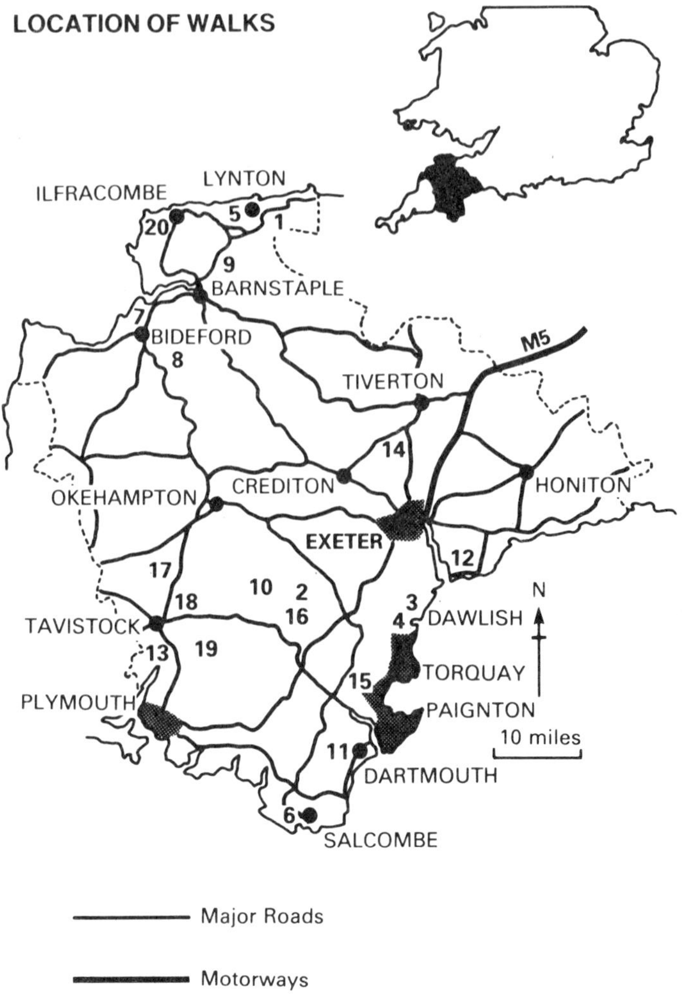

WALK 1
LITERARY
LORNA DOONE COUNTRY

(Oare Common – Malmsmead Hill)

MAP:	Ordnance Survey 'Landranger' sheet 180.
DISTANCE:	Nearly 7 miles (Malmsmead to the Doone Valley and return is about 5 miles).
ROUGH GUIDE TO TIME TAKEN:	$3\frac{1}{2}$ – 4 hours (about $2\frac{1}{2}$ for shorter walk).
TERRAIN:	Partly wooded river valley, partly high moorland. The first section is very popular in summer, the second less so, but both are clearly marked.
FOOD AND DRINK:	Refreshments at Malmsmead and Cloud Farm (summers only).
TRANSPORT:	Public car park at Malmsmead.
START AND FINISH:	Malmsmead (reached by a turning off the A39 near County Gate between Lynmouth and Minehead). Grid reference: 792478.

WALK 1

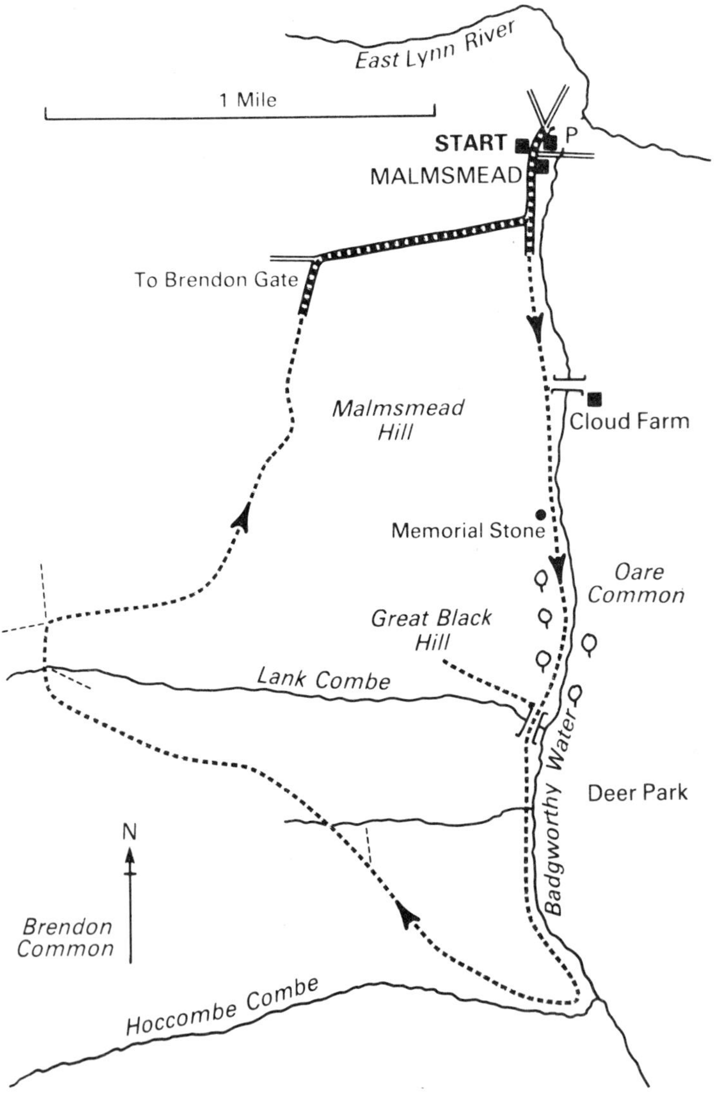
East Lynn River
1 Mile
START
P
MALMSMEAD
To Brendon Gate
Malmsmead Hill
Cloud Farm
Memorial Stone
Oare Common
Great Black Hill
Lank Combe
Badgworthy Water
Deer Park
N
Brendon Common
Hoccombe Combe

Lorna Doone, the most famous of R. D. Blackmore's novels, is set on Exmoor, at the easternmost edge of Devon. Here, in 'a deep green valley, carved from out the mountains in a perfect oval, and with a fence of sheer rock round it', which was how he described Hoccombe Combe where it runs into Badgworthy Water, Blackmore set the settlement of fourteen cots where lived the notorious, murderous Doones.

Blackmore's tale was pure fiction, though it was based on stories, part fact and mostly legend, which had circulated in Devon for generations about a gang of robbers and murderers who had terrorised Exmoor in the 17th century. At this period, Exmoor was a wild place. There were no well-built roads linking neatly fenced farms; instead, a barren wilderness overgrown with heather made excellent territory for villains to go to ground in.

Today, as anyone following the route of this walk will discover, the countryside of the Doones, though still wild and lonely, is no longer a place of terror.

From the Malmsmead car park, the walk turns left and goes towards the Lorna Doone Riding Stables. Ignoring the path signposted 'Short cut to Doone valley', keep to the right of the stables, carrying on along the road a short distance to a gate indicated by a yellow waymark and a sign 'Public bridleway to Doone Valley'. Through the gate, the clearly defined path drops down towards Badgworthy Water, keeping a little inland of the river, until it joins the 'Short Cut' path, ignored at the outset of the walk, near Cloud Farm.

After Cloud Farm, which is on the opposite bank and reached by a bridge, is passed, the valley widens and the path is through attractive woodland for a short distance until it comes out on to open, level ground.

Here, you will see the memorial stone to R. D. Blackmore, the man who ensured this walk – or at least this section of it – its enormous summertime popularity.

Past the memorial stone, you once again walk into woodland, where you may spot quite a large variety of birds; along the water, birds to watch out for include the dipper, grey wagtail and redstart. The land on the far (left-hand) bank of Badgworthy Water is Oare Common, and to the right and ahead rises Great Black Hill. At Yealcombe Water, flowing down into Badgworthy Water on one's right, is a gate to be negotiated, then the walk carries on through woodland, which becomes denser as one penetrates it; soon Lank Combe can be seen flowing through coniferous woods on the far bank and into Badgworthy Water.

After a short distance, the path emerges from oak woods to reach the footbridge over Lank Combe.

Lorna Doone fans wanting to see the inspiration for Blackmore's 'Water Slide' – three slabs of stepped rocks which the water slips over – can make a short detour here by turning right and walking 20 yards or so up Lank Combe.

To continue with the walk, cross the footbridge and follow the path through the rocky area of the Withycombe Ridge Water to reach a junction of paths. Take the path which turns right and goes up the Hoccombe Valley for half a mile to Brendon Common.

This is the valley of the Doones, where there is enough evidence of habitation – a ruined cottage, over-grown boundaries outlining former fields, and a widening of the path itself – to indicate that people certainly lived here at one time: perhaps the Doones themselves?

(The walk thus far will have taken about one and a quarter hours and covered some two and a half miles. It is a good enough introduction to Doone territory for those not wanting too long a walk to turn back here and retrace their way to Malmsmead.)

Continuing with the longer, circular route, you should follow the track, which is a bridleway, on up the Hoccombe Valley, through a gateway and so up on to Withycombe Ridge. The path, reasonably distinct for most of this section, climbs steadily through wind-swept bracken and heather (gloriously purple in autumn), crosses a stream and passes through a second gate in a wall at what is about the highest point on this walk – about 1,200 feet above sea level – before curving down a valley side to cross Lank Combe again.

Over the far side of the Combe, climb up the opposite slope, at whose summit is a signpost: the route for this walk is the way signposted 'Malmsmead'. The track slopes down to cross a stream, on the far side of which it broadens out into a gravelled way, and, as it climbs across the slope of Malmsmead Hill, offers splendid views in fine weather of the Bristol Channel and the coast of Wales beyond.

Soon the track comes to a metalled road. Turn right here to follow the road downhill, over a cattle grid, and so back to Malmsmead. (If you wish to avoid the road, you may cross over it, go through the gate here, and turn right to take the field path back to Malmsmead.)

WALK 2
LITERARY
GALSWORTHY'S MANATON AND THE HOUND OF THE BASKERVILLES

(Wingstone – Swallerton Gate – Hound Tor)

MAP:	Ordnance Survey 'Landranger' sheet 191.
DISTANCE:	About $6\frac{1}{2}$ miles.
ROUGH GUIDE TO TIME TAKEN:	$3\frac{1}{2}$ hours.
TERRAIN:	Moderately easy walk, mostly over rolling moorland, though with steep gradients in places.
FOOD AND DRINK:	Pub and general store in Manaton.
TRANSPORT:	Car park below St. Winifred's Church in Manaton (just off the B3344).
START AND FINISH:	Car park (as above). Grid reference: 750812.

WALK 2

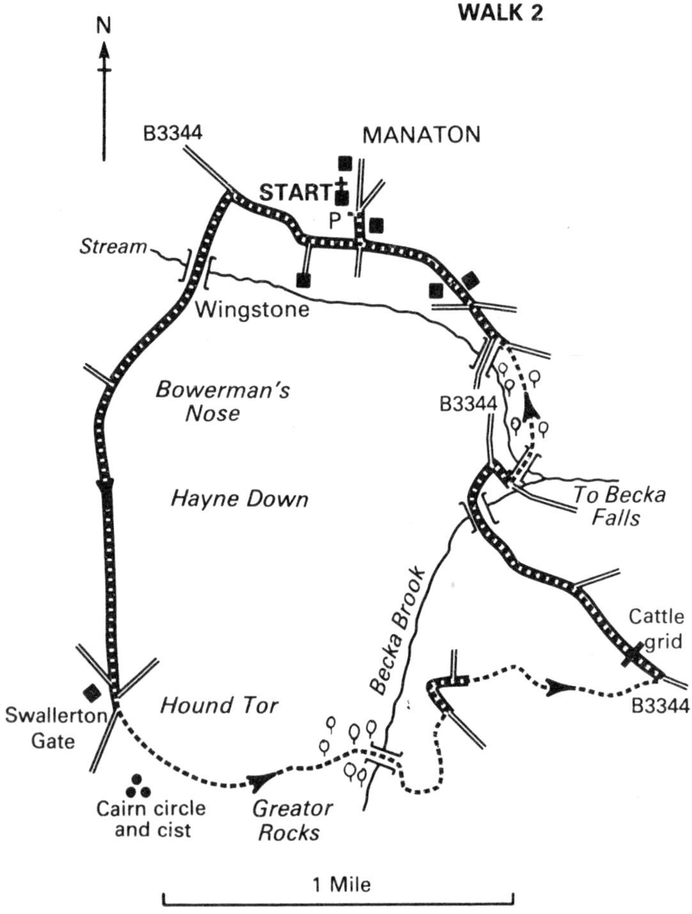
N
B3344
MANATON
START
P
Stream
Wingstone
Bowerman's Nose
B3344
Hayne Down
To Becka Falls
Becka Brook
Cattle grid
Swallerton Gate
Hound Tor
B3344
Cairn circle and cist
Greator Rocks
1 Mile

Manaton is a delightfully unspoilt Dartmoor village with a pretty green edged by an avenue of trees, and a church, St. Winifred's, which contains fine stained glass dating from the 15th century. John Galsworthy, the Nobel Prize-winning author, though born in Surrey, was of a Devonshire family and discovered Wingstone Farm on the edge of Manaton during a walking tour. He honeymooned there in 1904, and spent most of his summers there from 1906, when *A Man of Property*, the first book in *The Forsyte Saga* sequence was published, until 1923.

South of Manaton is magnificent moorland country, notable for its tors and rocky outcrops, including Bowerman's Nose, a stack of granite slabs with a distinctive 'nose' profile which takes its name from a man turned to stone by local witches, and the jagged Hound Tor. This tor was the one which Sir Arthur Conan Doyle provided with a phantom hound from Hell in *The Hound of the Baskervilles.* The hound killed the bad Sir Hugo Baskerville, for whom Conan Doyle got his inspiration from Sir Richard Cabell of Brooke Manor, an evil man who died in 1677. Black dogs (hell-hounds?) were said to have come racing in from the moors to howl at his corpse in Buckfastleigh Church.

Outside the car park the walk turns right, then right again on to the narrow B3344. After about 300 yards, a tree-lined drive leaves the road to the left, leading to Wingstone, Galsworthy's house.

The walk continues along the B3344 and takes the next turning on the left, a deep, narrow lane, following the lane down the hill, across a small stream and passing through a gate on to the moor. The road, now unfenced, climbs steeply up and around Bowerman's Nose. The views opening up behind are very fine. As Bowerman's Nose is passed on the left, the gradient eases and suddenly the rugged profile of Hound Tor appears against the skyline.

The walk now passes through another gate, labelled

'Moyles Gate', and continues along the road; a view across to Black Hill opens up on the left, with Hound Tor still dominating the view ahead.

At the end of the lane, you turn left opposite a very pretty thatch and stone cottage; a few yards further on is Swallerton Gate, a road junction and car park. You follow the road round to the right, then immediately strike out to the left across the moor, climbing gently upwards and keeping Hound Tor about 75 yards to the left. Towards the brow of the hill, a cairn circle and cist (stone coffin) will be seen. Once over the brow of the moor, head down towards Greator Rocks and the gap in the wall which runs from left to right in front of the rocks. Pass through the gap and bear left down the hill, keeping Greator Rocks on the right. The path is better marked now; pass through a gap in another wall, then head for the gate amongst the rocks on the skyline. The path then continues downwards, through a gateway, then steeply down the edge of a forest on the left. At the bottom of the valley, the path crosses the Becka Brook by a bridge of stone slabs.

Now the walk passes through a gate, then climbs up a rocky path through low scrub and woodland, finally emerging once again on to the open moor. Here, the walk turns to the left at the signpost and follows the path through bracken along the edge of Haytor Down. You pass into a clump of trees, cross a stone stile, then head up across the field to the gateway in the top corner. Note the fine views to the left back to Hound Tor and across to Hayne Down (Bowerman's Nose).

Once through the gateway, the walk turns left down a rough track, passes through another gate and rounds the corner to another signpost. You keep straight ahead up the hill, go through another gate, then continue to climb steeply up through the bracken. Soon the path becomes a stony track, the gradient eases, and superb views open up on the left, back towards Manaton. Skirting the edge of Black Hill, the walk follows the track which crosses open moorland before joining the road, at which point there are further fine views ahead.

At the road, the walk turns left and off the moor across a cattle grid. As the road goes downward, the gradient becomes very steep in places and the lane is buried between characteristically steep Devon banks. At the bottom of the hill, the road crosses the Becka Brook once again, and soon rejoins the B3344. You turn right here; 150 yards further on is the car park for Becka Falls which may be visited by following the well-marked route much frequented by visitors. If the weather has been dry for some time, the falls will probably not be much more than a trickle.

Returning to the B3344, you retrace your steps a short distance, then, just across the bridge over the brook, there is a footpath on the right leading into a wood which you follow, through the wood, crossing two stiles, then across a field to a gate and stile which leads back on to the road. Turn right to follow the B3344 back to Manaton and the car park.

WALK 3
LITERARY
JANE AUSTEN AND DICKENS AT DAWLISH

(Dawlish Water – Gatehouse Hill – Brunswick Place)

MAP:	Ordnance Survey 'Landranger' sheet 192.
DISTANCE:	About $5\frac{1}{4}$ miles.
ROUGH GUIDE TO TIME TAKEN:	3 hours.
TERRAIN:	Moderately easy walking, with some steep sections in river valley and hill country above Dawlish.
FOOD AND DRINK:	Cafés and pubs in Dawlish.
TRANSPORT:	Car park beside Dawlish Museum in Barton Terrace.
START AND FINISH:	By Dawlish Museum (open daily May–Sept). Grid reference: 958768.

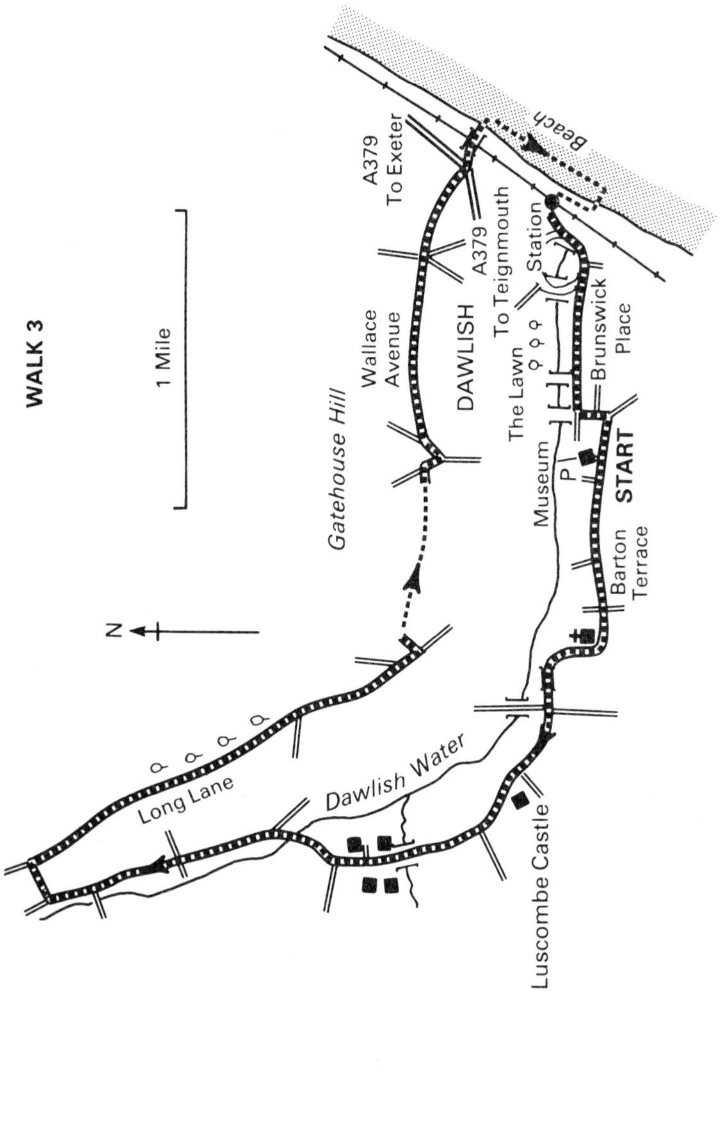
WALK 3
1 Mile
N
Gatehouse Hill
Wallace Avenue
DAWLISH
A379 To Exeter
A379 To Teignmouth
Station
Beach
The Lawn
Brunswick Place
Museum
P
START
Barton Terrace
Dawlish Water
Long Lane
Luscombe Castle

Described in a recent guide book as 'a sedate watering place' – a description well suited to Jane Austen, who liked the place very much – Dawlish was a fishing village which was turned into a seaside resort town late in the 18th century, and Jane Austen, holidaying here in 1802, would have seen the beginning of the building work which resulted in The Lawn, now a lovely park, which was laid out beside Dawlish Water the following year, and the elegant rows of Regency villas which still characterise the old part of Dawlish. Certainly she was charmed enough by the place to make Robert Ferrars say to Elinor Dashwood in *Sense and Sensibility* that it seemed rather surprising to him that anybody could live in Devonshire, without living near Dawlish.

Charles Dickens also found Dawlish an attractive place, and chose to make it – or at least a farm nearby – the birthplace of one of his more attractive heroes, Nicholas Nickleby.

From the car park beside Dawlish Museum in Barton Terrace the walk turns right into Barton Terrace. At the far end of the road, you keep straight ahead into the churchyard; keep to the right round the far end, going out through the lich-gate into an open grassy area. Here, the walk turns left along the path, through a gate, across a stream and out on to the road. Keep straight ahead at this road junction, noting to the left the castellated bridge over the lane which carries one of the drives of Luscombe Castle, a mansion (not open to the public) built in 1800–4 by John Nash for the banker, Charles Hoare. On the left is a picturesque cottage and the boundary of the castle grounds. Soon, the lodge and gates of the castle are passed, and, beyond them, the fine firs, cedars and pines of the Park can be seen. The walk turns right at the road junction, past a row of thatched cottages.

The gently undulating lane leads past Combe Brook, a fine Victorian house and farm outbuildings and on to

Rixdale Farm, a large, rambling, red-rendered farmhouse. Here the road veers right and crosses Dawlish Water by means of a ford and footbridge.

At the next junction, the walk turns left and follows the road along the gentle valley past several thatched cottages, beyond which the horizon is topped by the pine woods of Great Haldon. After easy walking of about three-quarters of a mile, you take the road on the right which climbs steeply up out of the valley. At the top, having admired the extensive views over the Exe estuary, you turn right along Long Lane.

Shortly, the metalled road becomes a track and climbs gently along the ridge of hills above Dawlish Water. The view on the left now embraces the whole Exe estuary, and the low red outcrops of Straight Point on the far side. The track levels out and passes beside a stretch of woodland; there is not much to see for a while, then there is a sudden view on the left across to Exmouth. Soon the road becomes metalled once more and drops down to a road junction, where you turn right.

After about 150 yards there is an opening and track on the left, and a gate and stile giving access to an open field. Keeping to the right-hand side of the field, the walk heads for the gate and stile, crosses the latter and goes through another field with extensive views to the left. Across a third stile is the summit of the walk, crowned by a ring of six lofty pines. The view is wonderful: to the left is the Exe estuary and Dorset coast beyond, ahead is the open sea, towards the right is the Devon coast stretching away to Tor Bay, and immediately below on the right is Dawlish. The early 19th-century kernel of the town sits in the valley of Dawlish Water, while the ranks of modern houses and bungalows spread up the hillsides. At the head of the town is the parish church near where the walk began. Behind, the view extends to the forests of

Great Haldon.

The walk continues on down the hill from the pines, alongside the hedge, then crosses a stile into a narrow tunnel-like path. Passing a range of glasshouses on the right, the path finally emerges on to Gatehouse Hill. Here you turn left, then immediately right into Wallace Avenue. Follow this road down the hill, past distinctly non-Dickensian bungalows; about halfway down, Strand Hill drops away on the right towards the town, between sheer walls of red sandstone. By now, the houses are getting older and larger – distinguished stuccoed villas.

Finally, modern blocks of holiday flats stand on the corner of the main A379 road. Here, the walk turns left, crosses the pedestrian crossing, goes a few yards back to the right and passes through a gateway and down a steep path to a footbridge over the railway line at the London end of Dawlish Station, built by Brunel to accommodate his railway line which reached the town in 1846.

At the foot of the steps, you turn right either along the sea-wall, or, if the tide permits, along the beach. At the far end of the station platform, built out on struts above the sand, turn right under the low railway bridge. Notice also that this is where Dawlish Water issues into the sea. Now you make your way across the pedestrian crossings on to The Lawn, the central park flanking the banks of the stream, and walk up the left-hand side of The Lawn along Brunswick Place; at the top end of the road, turn left away from the stream and follow the road round into Barton Terrace to return to the museum and the car park.

WALK 4
LITERARY
RUDYARD KIPLING AT ROCK HOUSE, MAIDENCOMBE

(Watcombe – Maidencombe – the South Devon Coast Path)

MAP:	Ordnance Survey 'Landranger' sheet 202.
DISTANCE:	About $4\frac{1}{4}$ miles.
ROUGH GUIDE TO TIME TAKEN:	$2\frac{3}{4}$ hours.
TERRAIN:	A coastal walk, sometimes steep or on precipitous cliff-tops, on an often rough track, with some road walking.
FOOD AND DRINK:	Seasonal tea-room in Maidencombe, or carry a picnic.
TRANSPORT:	Car park at Watcombe, signposted off the A379 Teignmouth–Torquay road.
START AND FINISH:	Car park (as above). Grid reference: 923675.

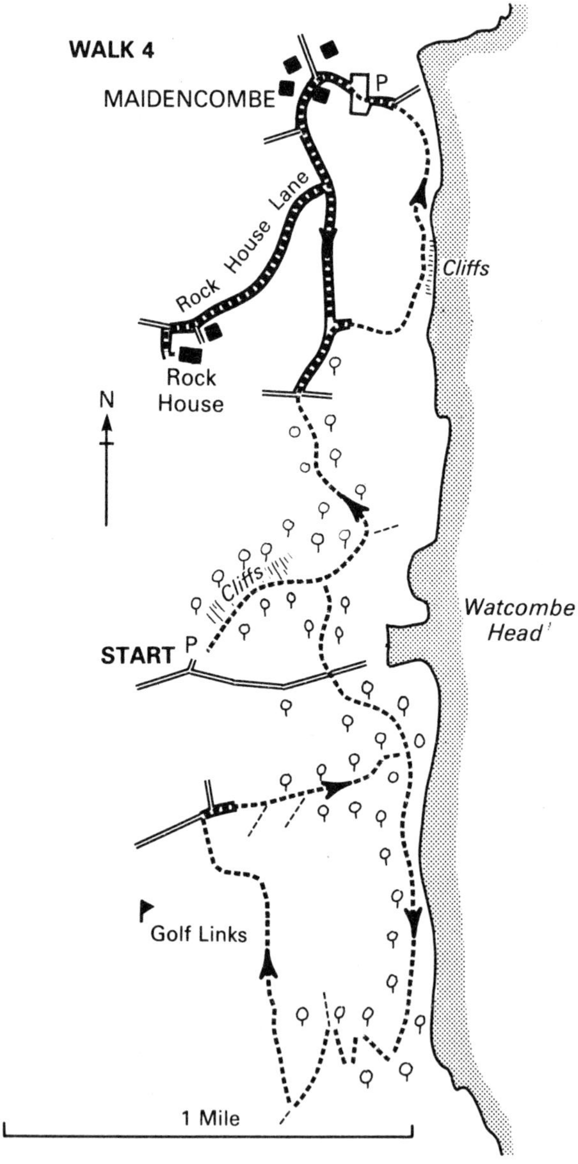
WALK 4
MAIDENCOMBE
P
Rock House Lane
Cliffs
Rock
House
N
Cliffs
Watcombe
Head
START
P
Golf Links
1 Mile

Maidencombe, the mid-point of this circular walk along the South Devon Coast path, is a district overlooking Babbacombe Bay north of Torquay. Here, in 1896, Rudyard Kipling and his wife Caroline discovered what seemed to them the perfect place – Rock House, down Rock House Lane – where the sunny aspect and the sea would surely provide the perfect atmosphere for writing. Less than a year later, they fled the house, driven out by the 'spirit of deep, deep Despondency' which Kipling said overhung the house and which had caused a dreadful depression in them both. Despite this strange manifestation of the apparently paranormal, Kipling managed to begin work on several books at Rock House, including some 'parables on the education of the young' which turned into the splendidly lively *Stalky and Co*, published in 1899.

The walk leaves the car park by a stile in the bottom corner, clearly marked for the Coast Path. The path runs down the side of a wooded gully, with sheer cliffs rising to the left. After a couple of hundred yards, a path branches off to the right – to which we will return later – but for the moment the walk keeps straight ahead. Soon the path begins to rise, and suddenly there is a fine view of the sea. The path climbs the side of the cliffs by steep steps; there is a handrail to help but this is on the inside of the path – there is nothing between walkers and a sheer drop except a few low shrubs, so take extreme care! At the top of the climb is a bench on a precipitous outcrop from which to admire the view, then the path turns north and downwards along the coast and back into woodland. Towards the bottom there is another fine view out to sea, then the path becomes a rough track and turns upwards once more. At the top of this rise, there is another junction of paths – to which we will, again, later return – but this time the walk turns right. The path heads down towards the cliff edge, then turns along the cliff, skirting a field. The walk follows the path on its switchback route along the cliff top, at times on the edge of a dizzy drop, at other times separated from the brink by trees and scrub.

Ahead you should now see Maidencombe, and before long the path emerges on to the narrow metalled road down to Maidencombe beach. You should turn up this road into the car park, past some public lavatories, then leave the car park by the road into Maidencombe itself. At the road junction, the walk turns left past the houses and a hotel, then at the next junction it turns left into Rock House Lane.

This lane climbs *very* steeply upwards, turns shortly to the right and continues upwards for about a quarter of a mile. At the top on the left is Rock House, its name clearly marked on the large castellated gate posts. Across the road from the gates of the house there is a very fine view north-eastwards across the Teign estuary and, beyond that, the mouth of the Exe and the Dorset coastline.

From Rock House, the walk retraces its way back down Rock House lane to the point where it turns sharply to the left; here, you turn right on to a rough track marked 'No Through Road'. This path climbs gently up along the side of the hill, the gateway on the left offering fine views out to sea. Shortly the walk meets the junction of paths already visited, and continues straight ahead to retrace the path all the way back down the cliff path to the first junction.

This time, the walk turns to the left and follows the path through woodland, at one point dropping steeply down a flight of rough steps. Eventually this path emerges on to the road down to Watcombe beach. Here, you turn left, then shortly right, back into the woods. The path climbs very steeply upwards by means of winding steps until the summit is reached, then becomes a broad walk dropping gently down through the trees, giving occasional views of the red cliffs of Watcombe Head breaking away into the sea. Another flight of steps leads up to another junction of paths to which, once again, we will return later.

Now the walk bears to the left, down some more steps, then southwards along the cliff edge. Ahead is a fine view of the coast towards Torquay and beyond. The switchback course of the path ends when it abruptly turns inland and climbs steeply by a series of dog-legs to join another path running along the hillside. Here, you turn left and shortly emerge from the wood at an oblique junction of paths from where there is a wide view of the Torquay suburbs of St. Marychurch and Babbacombe. The walk turns sharply up to the right, passes through a hedge and out into a high open field, where it passes through another hedge. A few yards further on is a bench commanding the finest views of the whole walk from a height of some 125 metres (about 400 feet).

The path leaves the field and turns to the left, skirts the edge of the golf links, then to the right, and, across a further open space, joins a metalled lane. Here the walk turns right, then bears right, through some metal railings on to a path that heads downwards once more towards the sea. After several flights of steps through a wood, the path rejoins our original path. From here, you retrace the walk down the steep steps to the Watcombe beach road; turn left up the steep lane and shortly you will arrive at the car park on the right, and the end of the walk.

WALK 5
LITERARY
SHELLEY AND THE VALLEY OF THE ROCKS

(Lynton – Lynmouth)

MAP:	Ordnance Survey 'Landranger' sheet 180.
DISTANCE:	About $4\frac{1}{4}$ miles.
ROUGH GUIDE TO TIME TAKEN:	$2\frac{3}{4}$ miles.
TERRAIN:	Moderately easy cliff-top and hill walking, a little steep in places.
FOOD AND DRINK:	Numerous cafés, tearooms in Lynton and Lynmouth.
TRANSPORT:	Public car parks (sign-posted in Lynton).
START AND FINISH:	Lynton town centre, near the Valley of the Rocks Hotel. Grid reference: 720496.

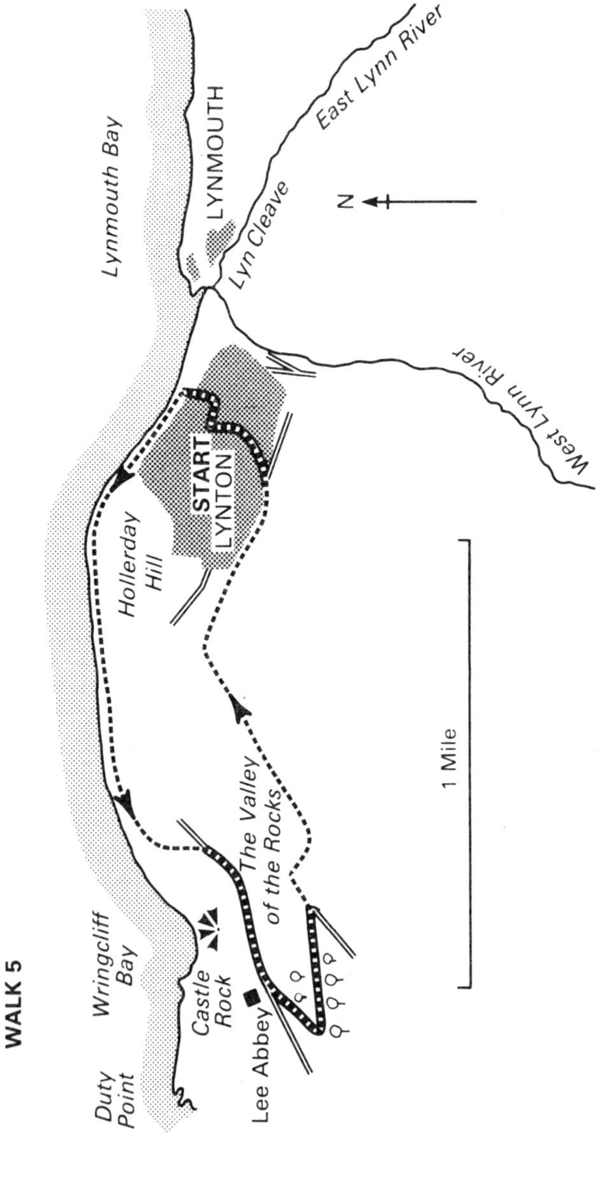
WALK 5
Lynmouth Bay
LYNMOUTH
East Lynn River
Lyn Cleave
N
West Lynn River
START
LYNTON
Hollerday Hill
The Valley of the Rocks
1 Mile
Wringcliff Bay
Castle Rock
Duty Point
Lee Abbey

The Valley of the Rocks, marked by rock pinnacles weathered into bizarre shapes and forms, is near enough to the twin North Devon towns of Lynton and Lynmouth for its formations to be seen topping the hills above them. A good motor road goes from Lynton direct to the Valley of the Rocks, but the most memorable way to reach it is to take the spectacular coast path, called the North Walk, from Lynton. This walk was the preferred way of the poet Shelley, who honeymooned in Lynmouth with his young bride, Harriet Westbrook, in 1812. The couple spent over two months in Lynmouth (in a cottage which, although rebuilt after a fire early this century, is still called Shelley's Cottage), during which time Shelley wrote *Queen Mab*.

The walk here probably also helped inspire Coleridge's *Ancient Mariner*, for Dorothy Wordsworth recorded how her brother, William, and Coleridge discussed the ballad, which was to become the great poem, while walking here.

Among the several ways to the North Walk from Lynmouth/Lynton (including the famous 1890 cliff railway from Lynmouth), perhaps the easiest to find is the sign-posted route off the main street in Lynton. This is a narrow road turning down towards the coast by the right-hand side of the large Valley of the Rocks Hotel. Follow this way, past the church, and you will come to the coast path near the cliff railway.

The North Walk was properly cut out and laid over 150 years ago, and is a fairly level, sealed path which twists and turns around the cliff 500 feet above the sea, with spectacular views of the rocky coast and across to the Welsh coast.

After about seven-eighths of a mile the cliff path, on which you will very likely have encountered some of the large and handsome goats which graze here, reaches open land and greensward, with the Valley of the Rocks on the left and the famous Castle Rock immediately ahead.

Here, the walk curves left and then turns right on to the road which goes up the valley to the left of Castle Rock towards Lee Abbey. (There is a path up Castle Rock for those wanting a fairly adventurous detour.) You should follow the sign-posted 'coastal path' here, ignoring the path to Wringcliff Bay. On the way up the valley to Lee Abbey the walk passes the beginning of a track which goes off uphill to the left to Mother Meldrum's Cave, which featured in R. D. Blackmore's *Lorna Doone*; Jan Ridd came here to ask the old woman for advice in carrying on his love affair with Lorna.

Once at the Abbey (which was never an abbey but a Victorian mansion – now one of the biggest mixed religious communities in Europe) the walk turns left through the gate opposite the main, arched entrance to the Abbey. This track, signposted 'Lynton over South Cliff', zig-zags uphill and then turns left into woodland along the ridge of a hill.

After less than a quarter of a mile, the path emerges from the wood on to the bracken covered slope of a hill, passes through a gate in a post-and-wire fence, and then, after 250 yards or so, zig-zags sharply to the right to go up and over the hill slope, and down the other side towards Lynton, two miles from Lee Abbey.

Once above Lynton, there are several ways off the path and down into the town, and where you choose to come down will probably depend on where you parked the car. The way down back to the centre of the town is via Lydiate Lane.

WALK 6
A WALK TO BOLT HEAD

(Sharpitor – Bolt Head)

MAP:	Ordnance Survey 'Landranger' sheet 202.
DISTANCE:	About $4\frac{1}{4}$ miles.
ROUGH GUIDE TO TIME TAKEN:	$2\frac{1}{2}$ – $2\frac{3}{4}$ hours.
TERRAIN:	Cliff-top and hilly farmland walking, steep in places.
FOOD AND DRINK:	Refreshments at Overbecks Garden and Museum; three hotels on South Sands.
TRANSPORT:	Car park at Overbeck Gardens, Sharpitor.
START AND FINISH:	Sharpitor. Grid reference: 729375.

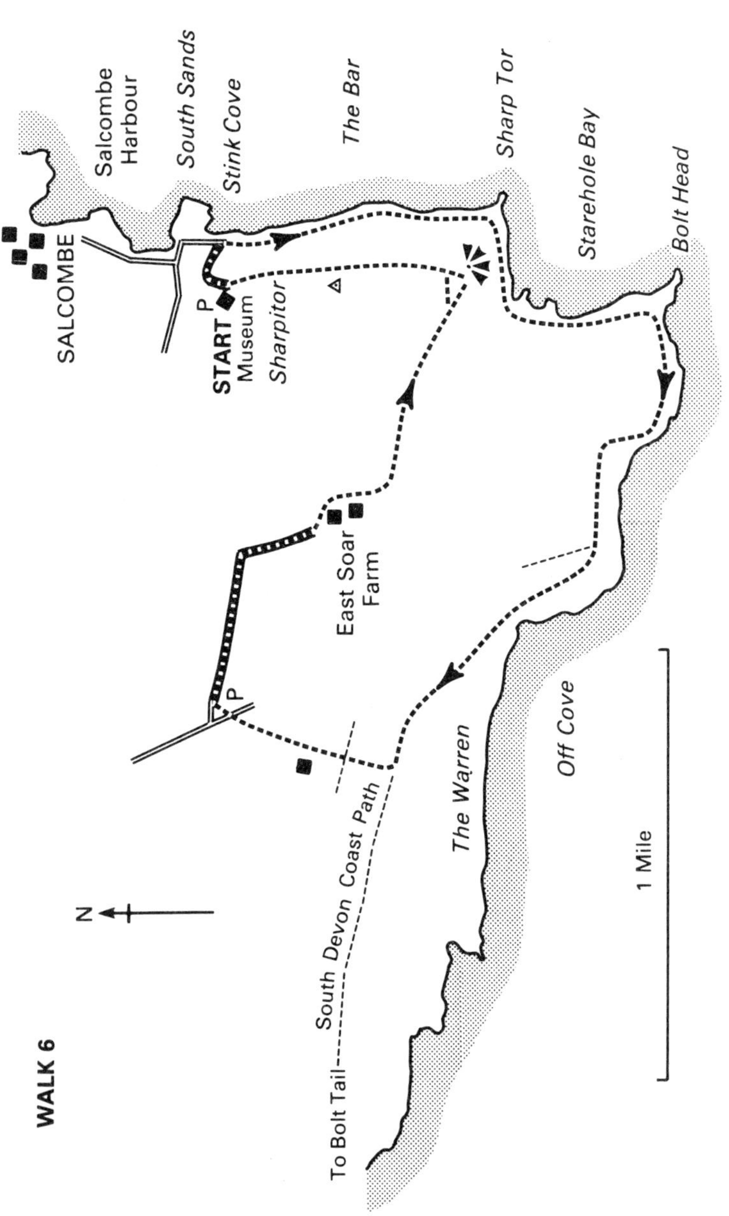
WALK 6
SALCOMBE
Salcombe Harbour
South Sands
Stink Cove
The Bar
Sharp Tor
Starehole Bay
Bolt Head
P
START
Museum
Sharpitor
East Soar Farm
P
South Devon Coast Path
To Bolt Tail
The Warren
Off Cove
N
1 Mile

The great Victorian historian and novelist, J. A. Froude, rented two houses on the land between North and South Sands in Salcombe for many years – first, The Moult, and later Woodville, now called Woodcot. In 1889, Alfred Tennyson broke a yachting holiday along the south-west coast to stay with Froude at Salcombe. He left on the yacht on a glorious evening in early summer. It was Sunday and the sound of church bells carried clearly over the water as the yacht sailed down Salcombe Harbour, across the sandy bar, where the waves swished and turned, and out to sea. Tennyson carried the impressions of the evening in his head for some months, until they bore fruit in one of his best-known poems, 'Crossing the Bar'.

From the National Trust car park at Sharpitor, the walk takes the lane down to the road, following the way signposted to Courtenay Walk and Bolt Head. The walk turns sharp right down on to the lovely tree-lined Courtenay Walk, where there are splendid views down through the woodland on the left to the sea and estuary below. Soon the downhill path comes to a white signpost indicating that the road ends here and the way beyond is a public footpath. The walk follows this clearly marked path, climbing quite steeply uphill now. After having negotiated a gate and a kissing gate on the path, and passed several seats, the walk comes to the lower side of Sharp Tor, where a railed viewpoint is reached by stone steps. From here, the views down to sandy Starehole Bay and of the jagged, rocky coastline are magnificent, with the Mewstone and Bolt Head showing on the far side of the bay. The sands of Starehole Bay are the graveyard of a Finnish four-masted barque, the *Herzogin Cecilie*, which struck the Ham Stone, west round the coast, in 1936 and foundered with her cargo of corn in the bay.

The walk now descends the cliff side of Sharp Tor, still following the clearly marked coast path, round to Bolt

Head, crossing a small wooden bridge over a stream which flows into the sea below Sharp Tor. From here, the path, close to the cliff edge, is very steep, but the views are marvellous and make the climb well worthwhile. Once the top of 420-foot Bolt Head is neared the path becomes much easier, with plenty of grass on the Head to relax on, and an observation point for an even better view of the coastline.

From Bolt Head, the walk follows the coast path west along the cliff edge, and keeps always to this path; ignore the path which goes off to the right beyond a stile you cross at the top of a grass-covered slope.

Just over half a mile from Bolt Head, the walk reaches Off Cove and The Warren, and carries on over a stile to come soon to a wall which reaches out to the path from the right. Beyond the corner of the wall is a path, which the walk now turns on to, to fork to the right away from the cliff path. You follow this path for rather more than a quarter of a mile until just below the derelict buildings of Middle Soar. Turn right on to the path which joins your path here, passing the buildings on your left. A few yards further on, go through the gate into a field, which the path cuts across the middle of to come out on a farm lane. Here, the walk turns left, arriving almost at once at a National Trust car park on the right. A signpost 'East Soar Farm', directs you over to the left-hand corner of the car park and on to a path which takes you past a coast-guard station, fenced off on the left, towards the cliffs.

After about half a mile, the path curves to the right, and the walk, passing a Youth Hostel sign, stays on the path to East Soar Farm. At the farm the path keeps to the left of the main buildings and negotiates a stile on the left-hand side. Once over this, the path keeps to the

'Lorna Doone Farm', Malmsmead (Walk 1)

AWL 962R

right-hand edge of the field, going through a gate just before the far corner, to continue on downhill to a junction of paths. Ignoring the stile and gate on the right, the walk turns left to follow a clear path through bracken and gorse and out on to another field where the path turns right, downhill, to negotiate a stile and wooden footbridge to come on to a broader path.

The land on both sides here is National Trust property, that on the left being fenced off and inaccessible to walkers. On the right, the land slopes to the cliffs and the views are splendid indeed.

Once on the broad track, the walk turns left in the direction of the sea and Sharp Tor. There are numerous paths off the clearly defined one of our walk, but if you keep always to the left you should not go wrong. After about three-quarters of a mile, the walk reaches the crest of 406-foot Sharp Tor, where the viewpoint indicator and the seascapes and landward horizon could hold your attention for some little time.

From here, the walk continues on the path to the left, with fenced farmland on the left and the Salcombe estuary to be seen on the right. After about a quarter of a mile, the path passes an Ordnance Survey triangulation point, and then drops down towards Sharpitor, passes over a stile and through a clump of trees, descending with the help of stone steps to a right turn into a rocky, tree-filled gully. About a quarter of a mile beyond here, the path leads the walk back into the Overbeck Gardens at Sharpitor.

South Sands, Salcombe (Walk 6)

WALK 7
LITERARY
A COAST AND COUNTRY WALK FROM WESTWARD HO!

(Pusehill – Abbotsham)

MAP:	Ordnance Survey 'Landranger' sheet 180.
DISTANCE:	About 4 miles.
ROUGH GUIDE TO TIME TAKEN:	$2\frac{1}{4}$ hours.
TERRAIN:	Easy hill, road and cliff-path walking.
FOOD AND DRINK:	Nothing on the route of the walk; several cafés etc. in Westward Ho!
TRANSPORT:	Car park in Merley Road or (especially at the height of the holiday season) in public car parks in Westward Ho!
START AND FINISH:	Atlantic Way, Westward Ho!, near Golden Bay Hotel. Grid reference: 429289.

WALK 7

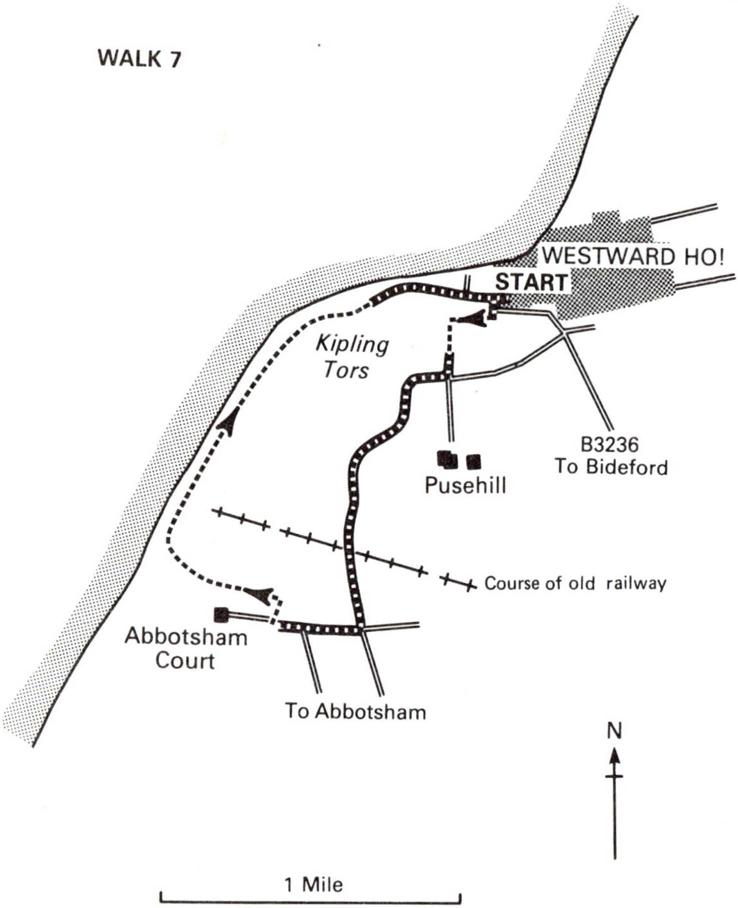
WESTWARD HO!
START
Kipling
Tors
B3236
To Bideford
Pusehill
Course of old railway
Abbotsham
Court
To Abbotsham
N
1 Mile

Despite the fact that this walk takes its name from the great novel of Elizabethan adventure written by Charles Kingsley in the mid-nineteenth century, its closest literary connection is with that great writer of Empire tales, Rudyard Kipling.

The building of the seaside resort of Westward Ho!, set on the tip of land north of Bideford, the town in which Kingsley wrote *Westward Ho!* in 1854–5, was begun in 1863, its planners no doubt confident that calling the resort after one of the most popular novels of the day would be to its advantage.

Rudyard Kipling's connection with Westward Ho! stems from the fact that he was educated at the United Services College there from 1878 to 1882. For 30 years the college occupied a terrace of 12 Victorian houses, now called Kipling Terrace, in the town near the coast path, along which Kipling used to walk with his school friends. He was to use his school experiences, including his coast path walks, as material for his schooldays' novel, *Stalky & Co.*

This walk's starting point is the public footpath going up to the National Trust-owned Kipling Tors from Atlantic Way, which is the Westward Ho! end of the B3236 road from Bideford via Buckleigh. Where, coming into the town, Atlantic Way turns sharp right (the large Golden Bay Hotel marks the corner), a left turn, Merley Road, goes down towards the coast path between the chalets and other buildings of Braddicks Holiday Camp. Outside August, this road is usually uncrowded enough to be a convenient place to park the car.

From Merley Road, the route of this walk takes you back into Atlantic Way, keeping to the right-hand side of the road. About 50 yards uphill, past the lockup garages of the Golden Bay Hotel and a disused stable block, a broad footpath goes uphill to the right. The walk keeps to this path, ignoring a path off to the left to a holiday centre. After another 50 yards, past a double garage, the path narrows and is lined with brambles. Already the walk is high enough up to offer good views across the holiday camp and up the three-mile length of the famous Pebble Ridge and Westward Ho!'s flat, safe beach.

About 150 yards uphill from the double garage the path forks, and this walk takes the left-hand way, which is quite steep now and through woods. Log steps in the path help make it an easy, though sharp climb, which soon comes out above the tree tops so that the views along the coast and out to sea are extensive.

Soon, the path meets other paths as a 'cross roads', our walk taking the left-turning path which goes uphill towards a familiarly-shaped National Trust sign with its back to us, indicating that the land here is part of Kipling Tors. A short walk along this path brings the walk first through a pair of white gate posts, with holiday camp and other buildings on the right and a footbridge on the left, and then through another gateway and out on to a sealed road.

Ignoring the road to Pusehill, straight ahead downhill, the walk turns right. The road, which is reasonably wide and set between banks and hedges – though walkers will need to keep well into the side to allow traffic to pass – takes up the middle section of this walk and offers splendid views over the north Devon hill farm country. At first the road goes gently uphill and has several houses along it, but as it curves round to the left there are fewer houses until the road is in farming country, and is running gently downhill. The downhill tendency of the road continues for rather less than a mile until it reaches the bottom of the valley it is crossing, where a line of trees stretching across the road marks the line of the old Bideford – Westward Ho! railway. From here, the road heads uphill again for about a third of a mile until it reaches a T-junction.

Here, the walk turns right (ignoring the left-hand

turning signposted 'Abbotsham'), and continues along the sealed road for another third of a mile (ignoring a second left-hand turning signposted 'Abbotsham'), until it ends at the gate into Abbotsham Court.

The walk now turns right to follow the signposted public footpath which runs along the Abbotsham Court fenceline for about 150 yards to a stile on the left, where a yellow and green 'Coast Path' sign directs the walk over the stile and on to the rolling tor and downland above Abbotsham cliff.

Although the path becomes indistinct after 100 yards or so, the way is easy: walkers should simply follow the line of the post-and-wire fence on the left until, after another 150 yards or so, they see a 'coast path' sign, set in the fence, and pointing downhill across the turf. Following the direction of the sign will take the walk downhill on to a distinct path leading to a wide stile and gate, on the other side of which is the Somerset and North Devon Coast Path. Turning to the right on this, the walk now follows the path back to Westward Ho!, $1\frac{1}{2}$ miles away.

At this Abbotsham point on the coast, the path is almost down to the level of the rock-strewn shore-line, but once the site of the old Cornbourgh firing range is reached, the path has begun to climb up from sea-level and is soon high enough to offer good views along the coast in both directions.

Soon the path turns inland slightly to go between the embankments of former railway cuttings, coming out abruptly round a corner of the cliffs on to the greensward below Kipling Tors. Following the path below the Tors, or cutting across the grass, brings the walk to the bottom end of Merley Road, at the far end of which is Atlantic Way and the start of the walk once more.

WALK 8
LITERARY
ON THE TRAIL OF TARKA THE OTTER

(Great Torrington – Weare Giffard)

MAP:	Ordnance Survey 'Landranger' sheet 180.
DISTANCE:	About 6 miles.
ROUGH GUIDE TO TIME TAKEN:	$3\frac{1}{2}$ hours.
TERRAIN:	Moderately easy railway line and country road walking, about one-third of it hilly.
FOOD AND DRINK:	Puffing Billy restaurant at Rothern Bridge in the former railway station building; Cyder Presse Inn at Weare Giffard (bar meals, pleasant terrace overlooking River Torridge).
TRANSPORT:	Car park at Puffing Billy, on A386.
START AND FINISH:	Platform of former railway station at Rothern Bridge, near Great Torrington on the A386. Grid reference: 480198.

WALK 8

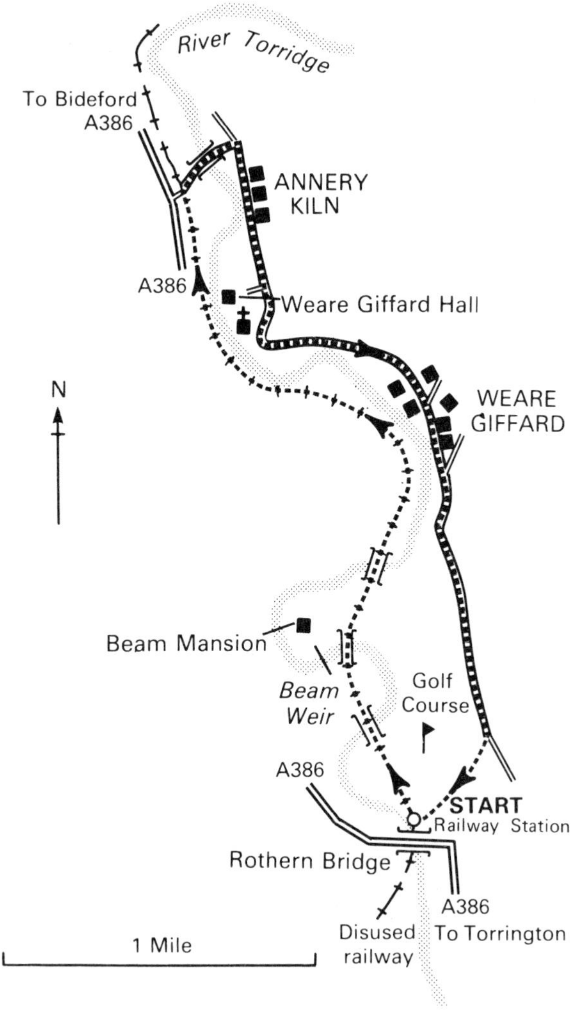
River Torridge
To Bideford
A386
ANNERY
KILN
A386
Weare Giffard Hall
N
WEARE
GIFFARD
Beam Mansion
Beam
Weir
Golf
Course
A386
START
Railway Station
Rothern Bridge
A386
To Torrington
Disused
railway
1 Mile

Henry Williamson's enchanting and moving story *Tarka the Otter* has been a favourite with children and adults alike since it was published in 1927. Set mostly in that part of North Devon watered by the Torridge and Taw rivers, the story tells of the life and dramatic death of an otter and of his relationship with the other wild creatures of the rivers' countryside and with Man, his constant hunter.

The first part of this walk, from Rothern Bridge to Weare Giffard Cross on the A386, is over a $2\frac{1}{2}$-mile section of the now disused railway line which first reached Great Torrington from Bideford in 1872. For most of the way the railway line is within sight or sound of the river which, on this stretch, flows north towards the Taw-Torridge estuary in a series of loops. For those acquainted with Henry Williamson's story, this is a particularly interesting section of the Torridge, for many incidents in Tarka's action-packed life, from his birth to his death, took place along it.

The walk starts from the platform of the disused station at Rothern Bridge on the A386, stepping down on to the tracks to set off in the direction of Landcross and Bideford (that is, from the left-hand end of the platform as you face the lines and keeping to the left-hand set of tracks, since the other sets soon merge and end at a set of buffers).

Short stretches of the railway line ahead are set between embankments, but for most of the way the views across the flat fields on either side of the Torridge, rising up to hills beyond the far bank, are extremely attractive and are marked by farm buildings, a large house or two and the villages of Weare Giffard and Annery Kiln.

The line crosses the river, high up on iron-railed bridges, three times along this stretch. Just beyond Beam

Weir, where Tarka and his sisters played, and where the wide weir and its sluice gate can be clearly seen from the railway bridge above, the railway also passes under a high-arched bridge which takes traffic from the nearby A386 into Beam Mansion, now a college, and which also figured in the Tarka story.

By the time the railway line reaches Weare Giffard Cross, the road sign for which can be seen from the track, the line is down on a level with and just a yard or so from the road, so it is a simple matter to step from the one on to the other.

Once on the road, the walk turns left to take the road signposted to Weare Giffard, doubling back under the railway line and, after 300 hundred yards or so, crossing the Torridge once more, this time over a picturesque hump-back bridge.

The next three miles of this walk are along this narrow, sealed road which winds its way along the eastern edge of the Torridge flat-lands (which are liable to flooding, so that there is no regular path along the river itself) and on the hills above.

Passing through the pretty little village of Annery Kiln, the walk keeps to the road signposted Weare Giffard, climbing uphill past houses and between quite high, hedge-lined banks until Weare Giffard's Holy Trinity Church is reached, set up above the road on the right and with a line of grave-stones peering over the churchyard wall rather like a set of teeth. Past the church and the walled grounds of Weare Giffard Hall, the road curves left back on to the flat land bordering the river, offering a foothpath on its left-hand side to take walkers into Weare Giffard village, just two miles from where the walk joined the road from the railway line at Weare Giffard Cross.

Through Weare Giffard, the walk keeps to the main road, now signposted to Torrington, and ignores the road on the left to Gammaton.

Beyond Weare Giffard the road climbs uphill between hedges and embankments again. After just under a mile the road has breasted the hill tops above the river and Great Torrington, offering fine views of the river and the hill and farm country around this ancient and historically interesting town.

Soon the fairways of the Great Torrington Golf Course come into sight on the right and it is here, just past the entrance gate to the golf course, that the walk leaves the road to take a clearly marked turning to the right on to an unpaved track wide enough for cars.

The track, which has viewing seats dotted along it, curves round to the left past two of the golf course's greens. The path is high up here, with the bracken and gorse-covered land dropping down towards the A386 and Rothern Bridge.

About a quarter of a mile along the track from the golf course entrance, a broad path – one of several used by walkers on this popular common – cuts off to the right through the bracken, and the walk turns on to this to return to the railway station, which is clearly visible on the road at the bottom of the hill.

WALK 9
HISTORIC
AROUND THE ARLINGTON ESTATE

(Ferny Park – Smallacombe Bridge – Barton)

MAPS:	Ordnance Survey 'Landranger' sheet 180; NT in Devon Leaflet No. 13, Arlington.
DISTANCE:	About $5\frac{1}{2}$ miles.
ROUGH GUIDE TO TIME TAKEN:	3 hours.
TERRAIN:	Woodland and hilly farmland, with short distance of narrow and quite steep country roads.
FOOD AND DRINK:	Restaurant at Arlington Court.
TRANSPORT:	NT car park opposite main entrance to Arlington Court (sign-posted off the A 39 north of Barnstaple.) Non-National Trust members must pay to enter Arlington.
START AND FINISH:	The beginning of the Nature Trail in front of Arlington Court. Grid reference: 612406.

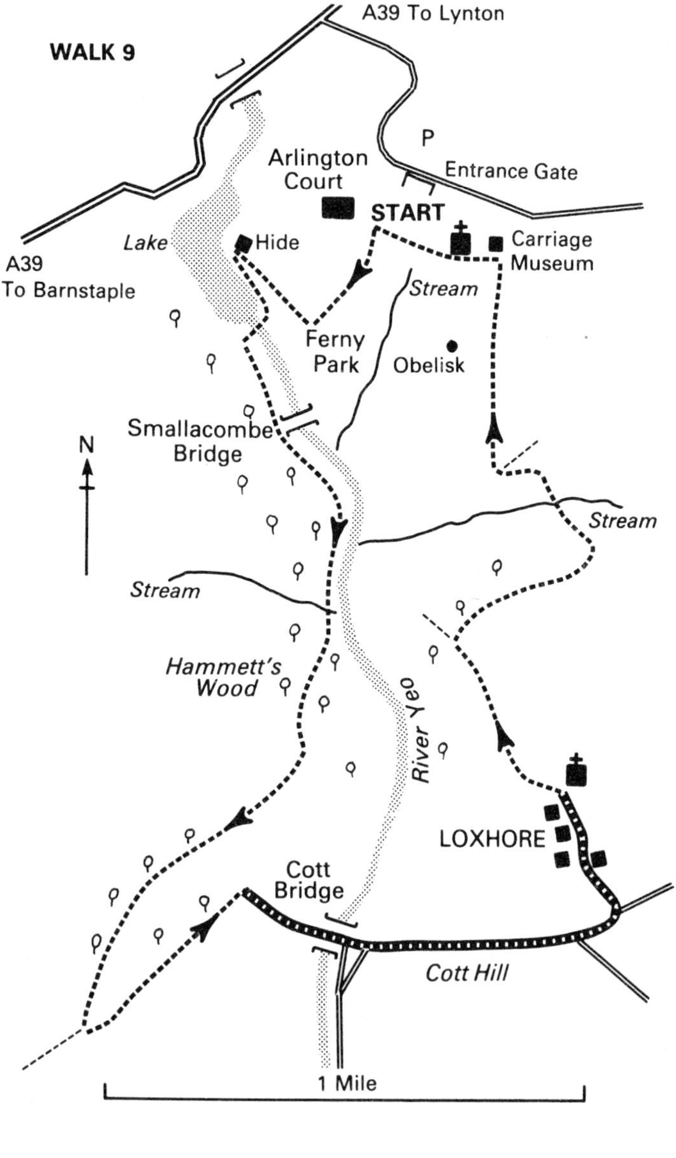

Salcombe Estuary (Walk 6)

Arlington Court, near Barnstaple in North Devon, is a particularly attractive National Trust property, once the estate of the Chichesters, a prominent family among North Devon's landed gentry. Although the estate came into the Chichesters' possession by marriage in the 14th century, the present relatively modest Neo-Georgian style house was built only early in the 19th century, replacing an older residence.

The house, gardens and grounds have been carefully restored since they were left to the Trust by the last Chichester owner, Miss Rosalie Chichester, in 1949. To visit Arlington is to step back into a quieter, more assured age than our own, for the house offers a splendid view of English domestic life among the Victorian country gentry. Outside, gardens, a park and farmland complete the estate, much of which was planted with woods and stands of rhododendrons and other plants to provide cover for game birds. Miss Rosalie Chichester, disapproving of shooting, turned much of the park into an animal sanctuary, and the descendants of her Jacob's Sheep, Shetland ponies and other creatures may be seen there today.

This walk explores the southern section of the Arlington estate, taking in both parkland and farmland and making use of the excellent Nature Trail laid out by the National Trust.

Having come out of Arlington Court by the front door (the main entrance) you should walk to the start of the Nature Trail, by the stile you can see next to the ha-ha which separates the garden from a section of the park. The walk crosses the stile and follows the clearly marked path, from which you should see Jacob's Sheep grazing, Shetland ponies and, after about 80 yards, a large beech tree, its trunk lichen covered and with a small hawthorn tree growing in the fork.

Soon the Nature Trail brings you into the pleasantly wooded Ferny Park, heading in the direction of the River Yeo. Following the trail, you turn right before the river is reached (ignoring a path to the left at the bottom of Ferny Park) cross a stile and continue along the grassy

The path to Bolt Head (Walk 6)

track, with rhododendrons prominent on either side, to reach one of the garden's carriage drives. Ahead is a hide from which you may observe the bird life on the L-shaped lake (created in the mid-19th century by damming the River Yeo).

From the hide, you should return to the carriage drive and then turn right to follow the lakeside path. The stone urn on a plinth which you will soon see on the right on a grassy clearing sloping down to the lake is a memorial to Miss Rosalie Chichester.

When the walk, still following the Nature Trail, reaches the south-east end of the lake, it turns right to cross the dam and then left to follow the River Yeo downstream through a lovely wooded landscape.

Soon, the Nature Trail turns left to cross Smallacombe Bridge over the river, but our walk continues on along the broad track (once a carriageway) by the river, following it as it curves round and passing on the left Tucker's Bridge over the river. Soon the track, having crossed a tiny stream, climbs up into Hammett's Wood, turning left, but remaining within the line of the woods, where the woods meet the farmland. After about 450 yards the track emerges on to farmland, stays on this for another 700 yards and then plunges back into the woodland of the Cott Down plantation.

The walk follows the track through the woodland until it comes out on to a narrow country road, which is part of the southern boundary of the Arlington estate. At the road, the walk turns left to follow the road along the ridge of the hill, turning right to come downhill over Cott Bridge over the Yeo and so on to the Barnstaple road.

The walk keeps left here, passing an Arlington estate gate, with the Chichester heraldic herons atop the posts; continuing on this road, you walk up steep Cott Hill towards Loxhore. This is a narrow road, sunk between high banks topped with hedges, so some care is needed, in summer particularly.

After half a mile, the walk comes to a narrow left turn signposted Loxhore Church, and turns down here to pass between the houses and farm buildings of Loxhore. Where the road curves to the right to end by the church lich-gate, a prominent public bridleway sign points to a path off to the left, and the walk follows this clearly marked path across the farmland back into Webbers Wood above the east bank of the Yeo. Once within the borders of the wood, the walk keeps to the broad track on the right, keeping to the edge of the woodland and following the track for about half a mile as it curves round to the left and then leaves the woodland, crossing another tiny stream, to come out once more on to farmland. This is the East Park of the Arlington estate, and is not open to the public, so walkers must remain on the path, being careful to shut all gates encountered on the way. You should keep to the path which turns left out of the woodland, ignoring a path which you will soon see forking to the right in the direction of Barton. The walk now follows the track north towards Arlington church and the cupola-topped stables (now housing the Arlington carriage museum). The obelisk you will see in the park to your left was erected to mark the site of a great Jubilee bonfire in 1887. Once at the stables, the path turns left to join the carriage drive back to the house.

WALK 10
HISTORIC
AROUND GRIMSPOUND, AN EARLY BRONZE AGE VILLAGE

(Grims Lake – Bennets Cross – Broad Barrow)

MAP:	Ordnance Survey 'Landranger' sheet 191.
DISTANCE:	About $6\frac{1}{4}$ miles.
ROUGH GUIDE TO TIME TAKEN:	4 hours.
TERRAIN:	Moderately easy walking over open moorland, though with steep sections. Since the path is sometimes faint and the walker may rely on seeing specific objects ahead of him as a guide, in misty weather the walk should be done only by experienced map and compass users.
FOOD AND DRINK:	Best to take your own; the *Warren House Inn* is a short detour from the walk's mid-point, however.

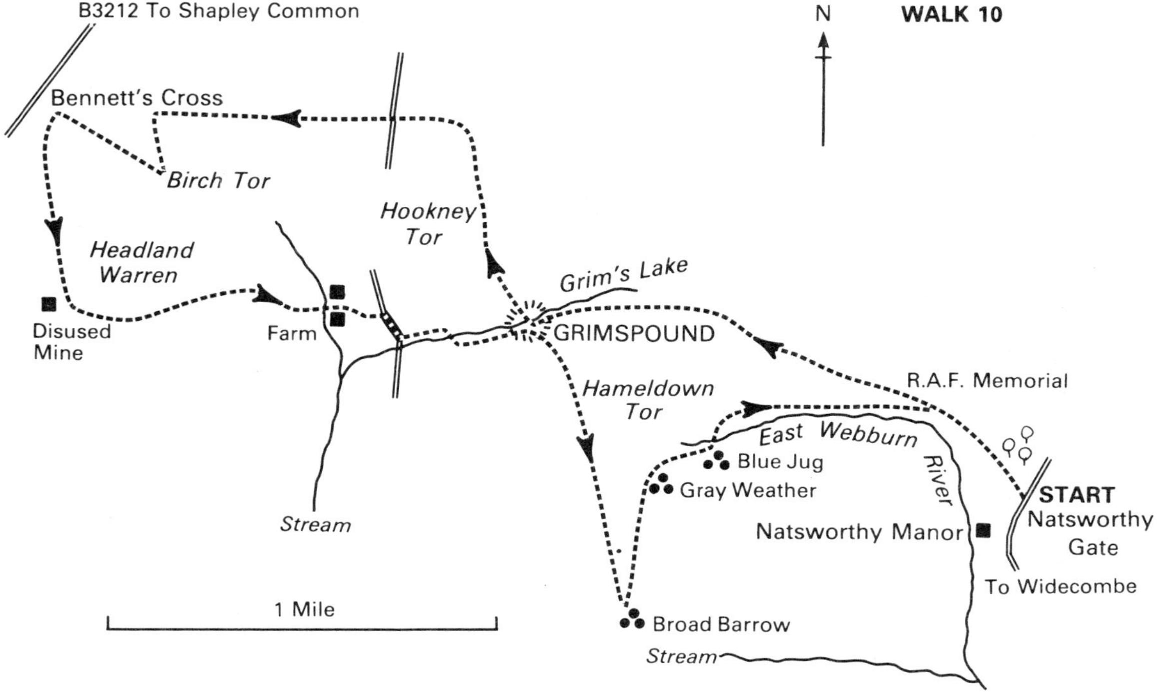
WALK 10
N
B3212 To Shapley Common
Bennett's Cross
Birch Tor
Hookney Tor
Headland Warren
Disused Mine
Farm
Grim's Lake
GRIMSPOUND
Hameldown Tor
R.A.F. Memorial
East Webburn River
Blue Jug
Gray Weather
START
Natsworthy Gate
Natsworthy Manor
To Widecombe
Stream
1 Mile
Broad Barrow
Stream

TRANSPORT:	On the side of the quiet minor road at Natsworthy Gate, just north of Natsworthy Manor on the road from Widecombe.
START AND FINISH OF WALK:	Natsworthy Gate. Grid reference: 721802.

The sight of Grimspound, the best-known of the Bronze Age pounds, or walled enclosures, on Dartmoor, brings pre-history and the Beaker People (so-called because of the shape of the pottery they made) very much alive for the many hundreds of people who walk to it every year.

Grimspound is a sizeable village enclosed within a great wall 9 feet thick and 6 feet high. Inside are 24 small, granite-walled hut circles, which would have been covered with turf or thatch roofs. Some of the huts clearly had protected entrance passages, and archeologists have found signs of human habitation, including charcoal from fires, in about half of them.

There is still a great gateway on the south side, built of dry stone masonry. Since the site looks indefensible, it was probably built by pastoral people not as a defence against enemies but to protect their sheep and cattle from wild animals, and could have been occupied any time between 2000 BC and 700 BC, and perhaps into the early Iron Age, c.450–250 BC.

The walk goes through Natsworthy Gate and on to open moorland, following a broad path up the hillside. There are several paths here, but so long as you stay on one going up the hill and not towards the woodland, you will be all right since the paths eventually come together.

Soon a pointed stone shows up clearly on the skyline, and the walk heads for it; the stone is a memorial to the crew of an RAF bomber which crashed here in 1941, and the stone was erected at the request of the mother of one of the four crewmen killed.

The walk carries on along the main path, which is slightly north of the memorial stone, in a westerly direction. The path begins to descend and soon reaches the Grimspound settlement, with Grims Lake, a stream liable to dry up in very dry weather, running through it. The views from up here are splendid.

From Grimspound, the walk follows the well-defined path which turns right (*not* the one which follows Grims Lake down to the road), to climb to the top of Hookney Tor, and carrying on through a gap in the stone wall ahead. Through the wall, the walk follows the path to the right down to the road, which is the Shapley Common – Widecombe road, reaching it by the end of a stone wall.

The walk now crosses the road to a path which climbs up through heather and bracken over a ridge and down the other side, to reach the roofless ruin of an old turf and stone building. Here, the walk follows the path to the left along a ridge to the summit of Birch Tor, which is clearly visible ahead. At Birch Tor the walk turns right to follow a clear path down towards the B3212, reaching it at a car park at Bennett's Cross. (Just half a mile down the road to the left is Warren House Inn, a good place to turn off to for food and drink.)

The walk now circles left, keeping the car park to the right, to follow the path downhill towards a point in the valley where several paths cross. The walk veers left along the main track, heading towards a cluster of old mine workings, which are passed as the path follows the lower contours of Headland Warren to Headland Warren Farm, which the path passes on the left-hand side. Past the farm, the walk follows the path straight on from the farm to reach the Shapley Common – Widecombe road again, though further south than the crossing earlier in the walk.

The walk turns right to follow the road a short distance until a car park is reached on the right. Here the walk climbs the steps in the roadside opposite the car park to reach a path which, crossing Grims Lake after a short distance, brings the walk back to Grimspound.

Rather than returning to Natsworthy Gate on the path it came up on, the walk now follows the path south (a right turn through the great gate at Grimspound), climbing steeply up to the 1737-foot Hameldown Tor, which has an Ordnance Survey triangulation pillar on its summit.

This is another splendid viewpoint, offering great vistas of much of North Devon, as far as Exmoor in the north-east, and of the country to the east as far as the Black Hills in Somerset.

From the tor, the walk follows the path south along Hameldown Ridge, passing the remains of Hameldown Cross on the right, and then continuing in a south-east direction down to Broad Barrow, a Bronze Age burial cairn.

Both these remains carry the mark of the mid-19th-century Duke of Somerset who once owned the land here; look for his initials DS on marker stones erected along his boundary.

This section of the walk – Grimspound to Broad Barrow – is on the Two Moors Way, which is quite well defined here, though walkers should take care to remain on it and not veer off on to one of the numerous minor tracks leading off it.

At Broad Barrow, the walk leaves the Two Moors Way, to turn sharp left to follow a good track north for about 400 yards, before curving right (north-east) into a depression in the moorland where is the head of the little East Webburn river. Here, at the top of an expanse of rushes, you will come to a boundary stone named 'Gray Weather' and, about 200 yards further on (north-east-north) down the slope, another stone, the 'Blue Jug'. The walk carries along the path, which is now following the course of the stream, but about halfway up the slope of the hill.

The walk continues to follow the course of the stream until, near the first of the trees which grow in the valley below the heather-covered moors, the path which runs up from Natsworthy Gate appears ahead. The walk joins this path to turn right and so come back to the start of the walk.

WALK 11
HISTORIC
DARTMOUTH CASTLE

(Blackstone Point – Warren Point – Little Dartmouth)

The walk takes in a section of the South Devon Coast Path and part of the National Trust's property around Dartmouth, offering superb views of coast, sea and countryside.

MAP:	Ordnance Survey 'Landranger' sheet 202.
DISTANCE:	About $3\frac{1}{4}$ miles.
ROUGH GUIDE TO TIME TAKEN:	$1\frac{1}{2}$ – 2 hours.
TERRAIN:	Well-marked cliff path, rocky in parts and gentle hilly track inland from coast.
FOOD AND DRINK:	Teashop at Dartmouth Castle, open most days in summer.
TRANSPORT:	National Trust car parks (sign-posted) on hill above Dartmouth Castle. (Walk may also be started near Little Dartmouth Farm, in which case parking is at the NT car park there, reached by taking the B3205 from the estuary road and turning right at Redlap Cross on to Redlap Road; car park is sign-posted.)
START AND FINISH:	Car parks at Dartmouth Castle. Grid reference: 886504

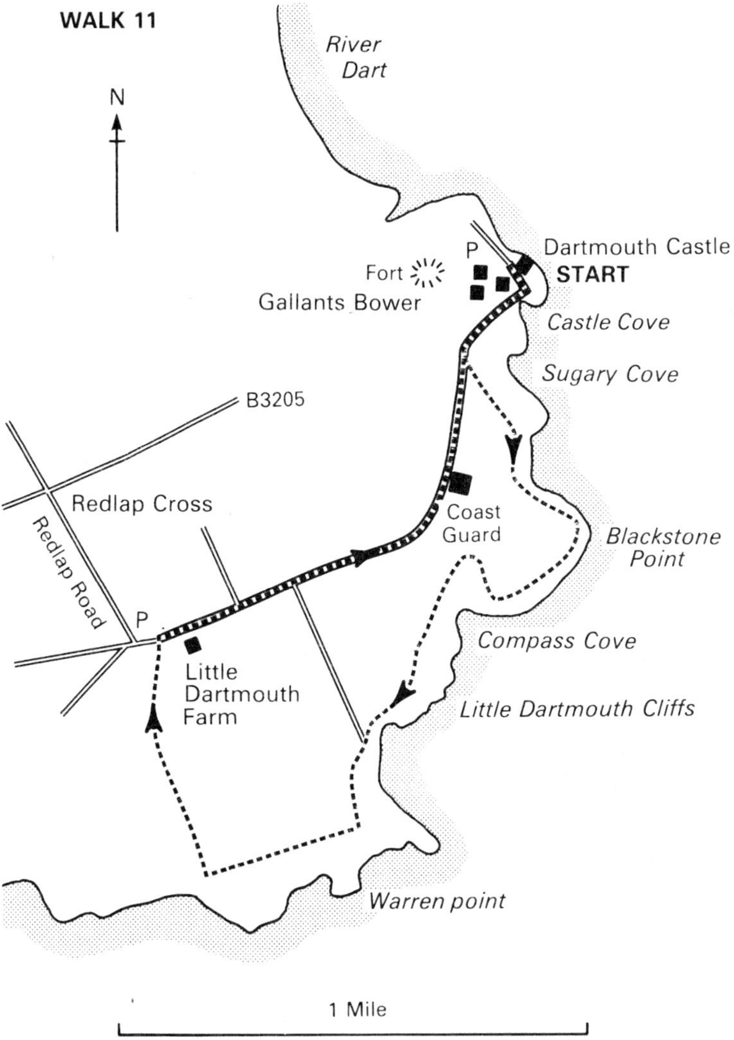
WALK 11
N
River Dart
Dartmouth Castle
START
P
Fort
Gallants Bower
Castle Cove
Sugary Cove
B3205
Redlap Cross
Redlap Road
Coast Guard
Blackstone Point
P
Compass Cove
Little Dartmouth Farm
Little Dartmouth Cliffs
Warren point
1 Mile

Dartmouth Castle, the object of this walk, has guarded the narrowest part of the Dart estuary since the 15th century. The ruins of its contemporary fellow guard, Kingswear Castle, stand on a promontory on the opposite shore of the Dart.

Dartmouth Castle was originally a simple fortification built in the 1380s against raiders and pirates from Brittany – this being the time of the Hundred Years' War – and there is still sufficient left of the later castle, including a round tower and its ramparts, complete with restored cannon, to give one a good idea of the site's strategic importance. Dartmouth Castle, which may be visited at the start or finish of this walk, is reached from the National Trust car parks by walking back downhill a short way to enter the castle grounds. The Castle and St. Petrock's Church within the precincts are open daily throughout the year, though the castle is closed at Christmas.

Note, too, in the car park area, the path to the right to Gallants Bower, once a Civil War redoubt and now a National Trust owned pretty woodland area, with good bird life, rising to 400 feet (120m) above the mouth of the River Dart: worth a detour.

To start the walk, head up towards the seat and the blue-painted iron fence ahead. Of the two paths here, take the right-hand path, signposted 'Compass Cove and Compass Hill'. You may follow the sealed road uphill to Compass Cottage, or go through one of the gaps in the stone wall on your left to follow a track off the road. At Compass Cottage, follow the coastal path (signposted by a National Trust wooden sign), which is sealed for a short distance until it passes the last of the cliff-top houses here; then it becomes stony. The path is within the Trust's Little Dartmouth property, which extends for one and a half miles along the cliffs west of the mouth of the Dart.

Soon the white-painted Coastguard buildings and mast rise on the hill to the right above one (though they are heavily obscured by trees and bush in the summer).

To the left, the land drops sharply down to the sea, and both Dartmouth and Kingwear Castles may be glimpsed through the trees, brambles and bracken which clothe the hillside.

Having rounded Blackstone Point, where a gun battery was placed in the 17th century, the path bends to the right to come down almost to sea level at a footbridge built over a narrow, sea-filled gully with caves cutting into the cliffs on the right. Once over the footbridge, stay on the right-hand path to reach Compass Cove, about half a mile from the start of the walk; from here, one of the first submarine cables was laid beneath the Channel to Guernsey in 1860.

From Compass Cove, the walk climbs up inland and away from the beach. (Ignore the side path that goes down to the cove.) Having crossed a stile, you follow the path gradually uphill, with bracken and gorse on either side, keeping to the left where the path forks so that you are always following the coast path. At the next stile, the coastal path is signposted; the path is high up here and the views are extensive.

The cliff path now passes round Willow Cove; once a stile and small footbridge have been negotiated, a Coastguard lookout point is reached (on the left). The National Trust have placed viewpoint seats in the field on the far side of a gap in the stone wall here.

The path now cuts across Warren Point, from where on clear days the views of Start Bay and Start Point are good. There is a plaque on Warren Point marking the contribution of the Devon Federation of Women's Institutes which helped the Trust to buy the Little Dartmouth Cliffs.

Beyond Warren Point, the path stays with the cliff for 200 yards or so before turning right to climb up gradually between fences towards Little Dartmouth Farm, negotiating on the way two stiles, the first of which has a notice beside it saying, 'Sheep! Please keep dogs under control'.

The second stile brings you into a lane, with the National Trust car park on the far side; here, you turn right to pass between Little Dartmouth Farm and Willow Cottage to reach the lane which takes the walk east over the spine of the hills, with farmland on either side, and back to Dartmouth Castle car parks, passing the Coastguard houses on the right and Compass Cottage on the left.

The South Devon Coastal Path

WALK 12
HISTORIC
HAYES BARTON AND SIR WALTER RALEIGH

(Yattington – Lympstone Common – Bicton Common)

MAP:	Ordnance Survey 'Landranger' sheet 192.
DISTANCE:	About $3\frac{1}{2}$ miles.
ROUGH GUIDE TO TIME TAKEN:	2 hours.
TERRAIN:	Hilly woodland and moorland walking, fairly steep in places, though never very difficult.
FOOD AND DRINK:	Sir Walter Raleigh Inn and Grasshopper's (tea, coffee, snacks) in East Budleigh; cream teas may also be available at Hayes Barton in summer.
TRANSPORT:	Large car park in woods on East Budleigh Common Road.
START AND FINISH:	150 yards from above car park. Grid reference: 042848.

Widecombe and the surrounding countryside (Walk 10)

WALK 12

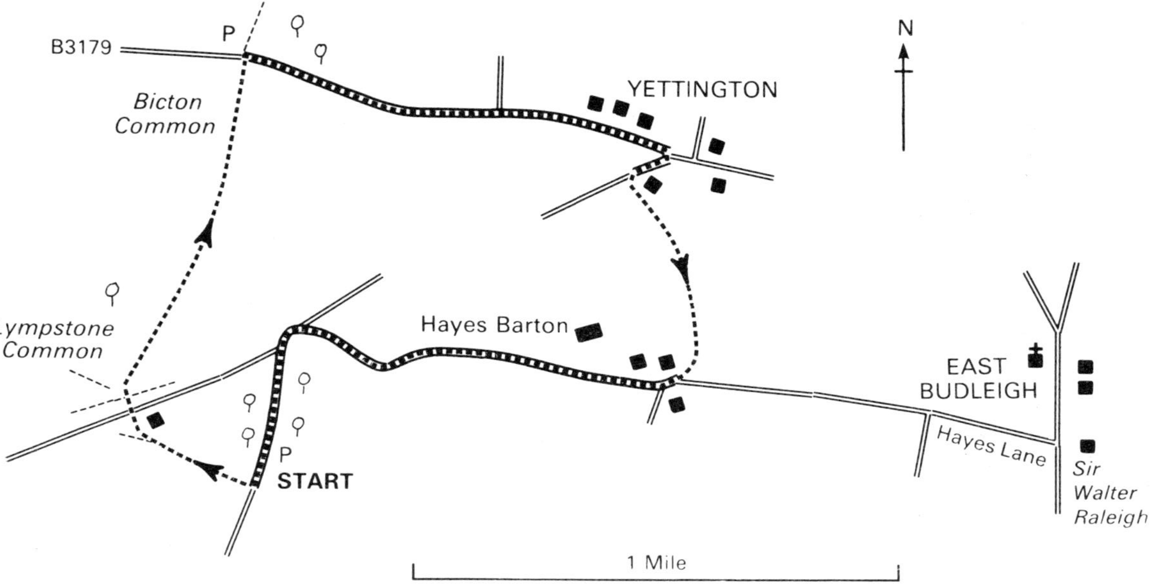

B3179
P
Bicton Common
YETTINGTON
N
Lympstone Common
Hayes Barton
EAST BUDLEIGH
P
START
Hayes Lane
Sir Walter Raleigh
1 Mile

Sir Walter Raleigh, the Elizabethan explorer, statesman and literary gentleman, was born at Hayes Barton, a Tudor farmhouse west of East Budleigh, in 1552. The house, a pleasant thatched and gabled cream-painted building, is still there. Now a private dwelling, it is not open to the public, though the owner, who does bed-and-breakfast in the season, may also offer cream teas in summer.

Beyond Hayes Barton lies wood and common land, very popular with walkers and picnic-parties in summer – and with the Marines, whom you may well encounter emerging dripping with camouflage from copses of bracken and trees, though they usually exercise outside the summer months.

To reach the starting point of the walk, drive to East Budleigh, which lies off the A376 north of Budleigh Salterton. From the centre of the village, turn on to Hayes Lane which goes off from the main street, High Street, directly opposite the Sir Walter Raleigh inn; the lane is sign-posted 'To the birthplace of Sir Walter Raleigh'. You drive along this typically sunken, narrow Devon road for about one and a half miles, passing Hayes Barton after a mile, to a T-junction. Here, you turn left and left again after 50 yards or so, to come on to a wider road through woodland. There are numerous small parking places, with notices asking people to observe the country code etc, off both sides of this road, but you should keep driving for rather less than a quarter of a mile until you come to a markedly larger parking area on the left. Here you park the car to begin the walk.

Since many walkers have tramped paths of their own through the bracken here, there is a maze of paths, seemingly designed to confuse anyone trying to follow a more precisely described walk. However, so long as you keep walking in the direction we indicate, you should not get lost.

From the car park, the walk turns left along the road

for about 150 yards. On the right, you should then see a reasonably wide path (about a yard), gravelled at this point and clearly defined, going off into the bracken. Our walk follows this path for about 600 yards, when it crosses a wider bridle path. Here, the walk turns right on to the bridle path, to reach very soon the sealed road which crosses Lympstone Common. The road is wooded on both sides at this point, and on the right (south) side, where the path meets the road, there is a brick shed with graffiti scrawled on the side. (If you do not see this shed it is probably because you missed the right-hand fork back in the bracken; if so, you will have come out on to the Lympstone Common road a hundred yards or so too far west, and you should turn right and walk along the road until you come to the brick shed.)

Once the shed is reached, the walk crosses the road to where a reasonably broad path goes into the wood and bracken, at an angle of about 45 degrees to the right. The walk follows this path, which very soon joins a bridle path; here, the walk turns right along the bridle path to walk across the slope of hilly, bracken-covered common land for about half a mile, coming out on to the wide B3179 road at Bicton Common.

Here the walk turns right and follows this road, which runs unfenced and mostly downhill through pleasantly wooded land for approximately a mile into the village of Yettington. Once in the village, you will very soon see a white-painted signpost on the right-hand side of the road. Here, you turn right, taking the road signposted 'Exmouth $4\frac{1}{2}$ miles' over a metal-railed bridge across a small stream. On the left, about 70 yards beyond the bridge just past a brick farm building, the walk comes to a stile by a wooden gate, with a 'public footpath' sign pointing across it. The walk now follows this path across farm fields, and round the hill which rises behind Hayes

Barton, to come down on to the road from East Budleigh by the farm buildings of Hayes Barton.

Once on the road, the walk turns right to go in front of Hayes Barton and follow the narrow, hedged road back uphill to the T-junction where the walk turns left and left again to reach the road where the car was parked at the outset of the walk.

WALK 13
HISTORIC
FRANCIS DRAKE COUNTRY

(Buckland Monachorum – Lopwell Dam – Mitton Combe)

MAP:	Ordnance Survey 'Landranger' sheet 210.
DISTANCE:	About $6\frac{1}{2}$ miles.
ROUGH GUIDE TO TIME TAKEN:	$3\frac{1}{2}$ – 4 hours.
TERRAIN:	Easy walking by riverside, on country roads, and some farmland walking.
FOOD AND DRINK:	Refreshments and café at Buckland Abbey, Easter–Sept, Drake Manor Inn at Buckland Monachorum.
TRANSPORT:	National Trust car park at Buckland Abbey.
START AND FINISH:	Main entrance gate to Buckland Abbey. Grid reference: 488668.

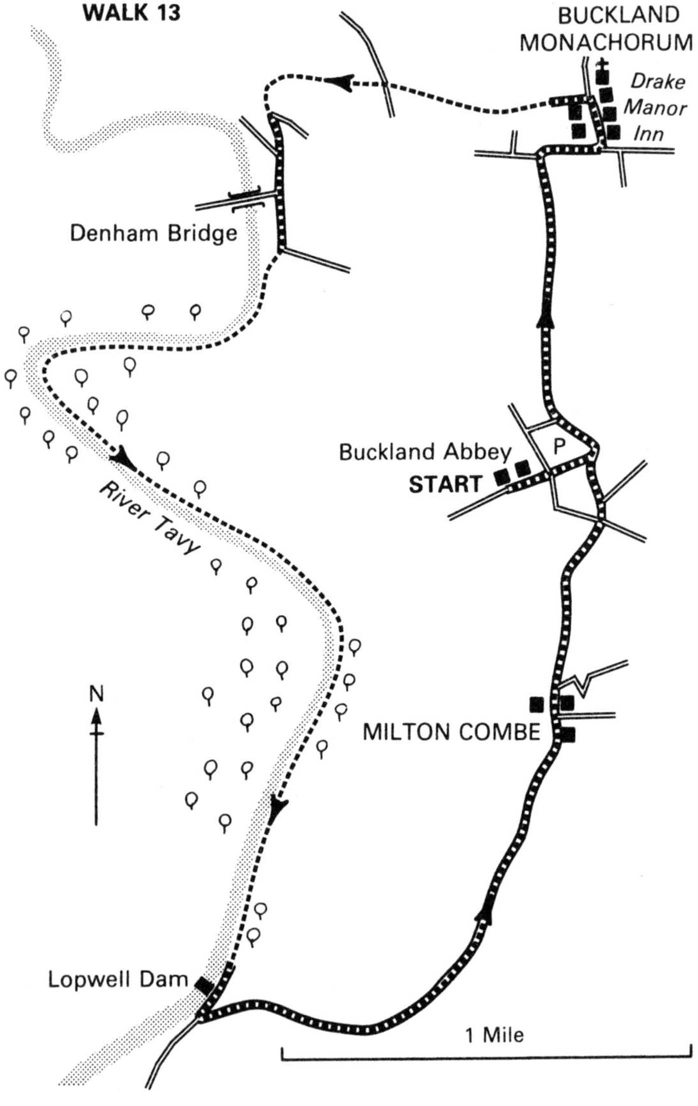
WALK 13
BUCKLAND
MONACHORUM
Drake
Manor
Inn
Denham Bridge
Buckland Abbey
P
START
River Tavy
N
MILTON COMBE
Lopwell Dam
1 Mile

Sir Francis Drake bought Buckland Abbey in 1581, after circumnavigating the globe, from his equally famous fellow-sailor Sir Richard Grenville of the *Revenge*. The abbey was originally a Cistercian house founded by a 13th-century Countess of Devon and was bought in 1541, after the Dissolution of the Monasteries, by Sir Richard's grandfather, also Sir Richard Grenville. The Grenvilles and Drake all had a hand in turning the abbey into a fine mansion, and today the place is a fine museum, owned by the National Trust and leased to the Plymouth Corporation. As well as collections of local Devon interest, the house also contains many Drake relics.

The house is set in lovely gardens where there are other buildings, including a splendid tithe barn, to be visited. Buckland Abbey is open daily Easter to the end of September; and October until the Wednesday before Easter, Wednesdays, Saturdays and Sundays (open p.m.).

This is a longish walk in the country around Buckland Abbey, taking in a stretch of the River Tavy and the interesting old medieval village of Buckland Monachorum a mile to the north of the abbey.

From the main entracen gate at Buckland Abbey, the walk turns left to follow the road north to Buckland Monachorum. After almost a mile, where the village outskirts are reached, the road comes to a T-junction, and the walk turns right here and then left to come into the village.

Almost in the centre of Buckland Monachorum is an interesting group of buildings, with the 16th-century Drake Manor Inn standing next to the fine parish Church of St Andrew, which retains an impressive interior dating from rebuilding work in the 15th and 16th centuries: look out for the Drake family monuments and a splendid Norman font.

From in front of the church, the walk continues by turning to the left to take, after 20 yards or so, the first turning to the right (the general store/Post Office is on the corner) down a narrow road. Just past the Post Office, the walk negotiates a wrought iron gate then a wooden gate to come on to a path through a housing estate and so on to a footpath leading across fields and farmland in the direction of the River Tavy.

After just under half a mile the footpath comes out on to a narrow road. Here the walk turns right then, after about 150 yards, left again down a farm track where the footpath is picked up again on the left just before the lane curves right towards the farm buildings at the end of the lane. The walk follows the path across farmland again.

After about quarter of a mile, the path becomes sealed and runs between low hedges down on to the Denham-Hatch Mill road.

Here, you should cross the road to the path, sign-posted 'public footpath', which crosses a field to come down on to a hairpin bend on the road which now runs down the east bank of the River Tavy. The walk follows the road, which has high banks and woods on either side, for about 100 yards down to Denham Bridge, an attrative stone structure with a pointed arch, beneath which the river runs 40 feet deep and where, according to a prominent notice, 'bathing is dangerous'.

The walk does not cross the bridge but carries on down the road, with the river on the right, for about 120 yards to join a footpath (not signposted but reasonably prominent) which goes off from the road on the right and winds its way through woodland to the river.

The walk follows this path downstream and through pretty woodland for rather more than one and a half miles until it is below the high walls surrounding the grounds of Buckland Abbey.

Since there is no way into the abbey grounds here, the walk continues to follow the river, with the path often much less distinct now but the direction still quite clear, for another mile until Lopwell Dam, at the head of the Tavy estuary, is reached.

Here, the walk comes up across the eastern end of the dam and turns right on to the road to Milton Combe, following a stream through woodland before curving across the slope of the hills of the Tavy valley to reach Milton Combe, just over two miles from the dam. Through Milton Combe, the walk continues along the road for about quarter of a mile to reach a left turning signposted 'Buckland Abbey'.

WALK 14
HISTORIC
BICKLEIGH CASTLE

(Bickleigh Mill – Bickleigh Castle)

MAP:	Ordnance Survey 'Landranger' sheet 192.
DISTANCE:	About $3\frac{1}{4}$ miles.
ROUGH GUIDE TO TIME TAKEN:	$1\frac{3}{4}$ hours.
TERRAIN:	Easy walking in flat river valley pastureland; some road walking.
FOOD AND DRINK:	Bickleigh Mill Craft Centre (open p.m.), Trout Inn Free House, Bickleigh Cottage and Fisherman's Cot Hotel, all near Bickleigh Bridge on A396.
TRANSPORT:	Car park at Bickleigh Mill Craft Centre.
START AND FINISH:	Bickleigh Mill. Grid reference: 939076.

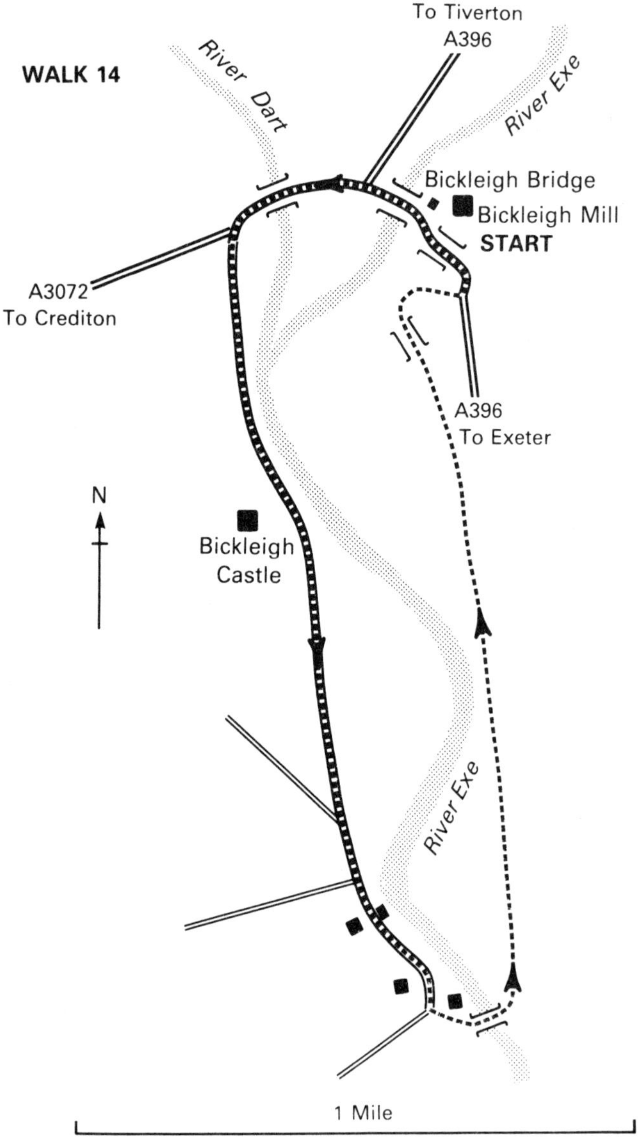
WALK 14
To Tiverton
A396
River Dart
River Exe
Bickleigh Bridge
Bickleigh Mill
START
A3072
To Crediton
A396
To Exeter
N
Bickleigh
Castle
River Exe
1 Mile

Bickleigh Castle, which lies quarter of a mile off the A3072 south of Tiverton, is a delightfully mellow-looking place, in a beautiful setting on the west bank of the River Exe. Back in Norman times it was a simple manor house, which came into the possession of the great Devon family, the Courtenays, whose main seat is still Powderham Castle near Exeter.

The Courtenays rebuilt and fortified Bickleigh in the 15th century, and you can still see the gatehouse and a section of the moat they built, though the former was rebuilt again by later owners, the Carews, in the 17th century. Under the Courtenays, Bickleigh Castle became by tradition an estate given to younger sons of the family and it is not difficult today, as you look at the hatched buildings and the clock tower with its cock weathervane on top, to imagine family life going on in this pleasant place.

Today, attractions for visitors to Bickleigh Castle (open Easter Week; Wed, Sun, Bank Holiday Mondays to end May; daily exc. Sat, June–Oct 2 – 5pm) include an armoury, Tudor bedroom, Stewart farmhouse, guardroom, tower, Great Hall and an 11th-century chapel.

This easy walk centred on Bickleigh Castle begins at another interesting place in the village, Bickleigh Mill, now a craft centre.

From Bickleigh Mill, the walk crosses the Exe over Bickleigh Bridge, an attractive stone structure in a lovely setting and dating from the 16th century. Just below here the Dart joins the Exe.

Over the bridges which cross the two rivers, the walk keeps to the left, curving round on to the A3072 in the direction of Crediton.

A couple of hundred yards down the road, a minor road sign-posted 'Bickleigh Castle ¼ mile' forks off downhill to the left, and the walk follows this. The sealed road is bordered on either side by bushes and magnificent old trees and closely follows the river until Bickleigh Castle is reached.

Past the castle, the walk follows the road south, now somewhat inland of the river, which is still in view across the green pastureland.

After nearly three-quarters of a mile, and having passed two turnings off to the right, the first a small farm road and the second a minor road going uphill via Perry and Chilton to join the A3072, the road and the river each curve in to meet each other again. Just beyond the second group of buildings the road now passes between; a path goes off to the left across the field here towards the river.

The riverside reached, the path goes over the river by a narrow suspension bridge – basically two sets of boards suspended between metal uprights – so that walkers are brought over to the east bank of the river. Here, turn left to join the path which takes you back to Bickleigh Bridge and the mill. The path is very clearly marked, following the course of a dismantled railway. Thus, it is on an embankment, fenced on both sides, above the level of the lovely pastureland which reaches to the hills which rise up in gentle, wooded curves to 700 feet above the river valley on either side.

It is a very easy, gentle and attractive walk, offering views of the middle Exe valley and of Bickleigh Castle, with only a bridge over a small stream and a couple of gates to be negotiated before you arrive at Bickleigh Bridge and the way back to the mill on the other side of the road.

Bickleigh Castle (Walk 14)

Peter Tavy
Inn

WALK 15 HISTORIC
AROUND BERRY POMEROY CASTLE

(Berry Pomeroy – Berry Castle Lodge)

MAP:	Ordnance Survey 'Landranger' sheet 202.
DISTANCE:	Just over 3 miles.
ROUGH GUIDE TO TIME TAKEN:	$1\frac{1}{4}$ – $1\frac{1}{2}$ hours.
TERRAIN:	A woodland walk, sometimes quite steep as the walk climbs away from the valley of the Gatcombe Brook. The route is clearly marked, sometimes following a sealed road, and mostly on woodland paths which may be muddy after rain.
FOOD AND DRINK:	A wooden chalet-style tea-room in front of the castle is open during the summer season.
TRANSPORT:	Car park at Berry Pomeroy Castle. The castle is clearly signposted from Berry Pomeroy village, on a minor road signposted off the A385.

The Peter Tavy Inn (Walk 18)

WALK 15

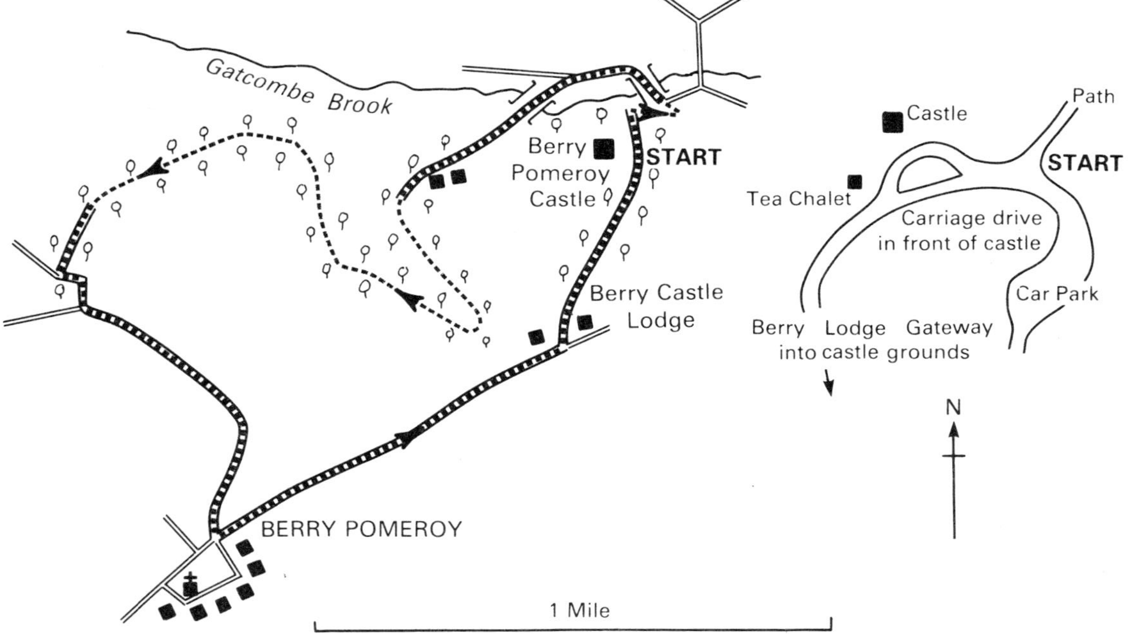
Gatcombe Brook
Berry Pomeroy Castle
START
Berry Castle Lodge
BERRY POMEROY
1 Mile
Castle
Path
START
Tea Chalet
Carriage drive in front of castle
Car Park
Berry Lodge Gateway into castle grounds
N

START AND FINISH:	Berry Pomeroy Castle. Grid reference: 839624.

This walk is in the countryside surrounding the romantic ruins of Berry Pomeroy Castle, two miles east of Totnes off the A385. The castle was probably begun in the 13th century by the de la Pomerai family who had owned the estate here since the Norman Conquest, though the remains one sees today are no older than the 15th century. In 1548 the de la Pomerai family sold the castle to Edward Seymour, Duke of Somerset, and it is his descendant, the 19th Duke of Somerset, who still owns it.

In the 17th century, the Seymours began turning the grim castle with its 15th-century gatehouse and great curtain wall into a luxurious mansion with a suite of state rooms; here, in 1688, Sir Edward Seymour welcomed William of Orange after his landing at Brixham. Not long after, the Seymours abandoned Berry Pomeroy Castle and it fell into decay, from which the Department of the Environment is now rescuing it.

With the castle gate at your back, turn left in the direction of the car park. Before the car park is reached, you come to a large beech tree and the start of the walk (signposted 'public footpath'). This forks off on the left-hand side of the road.

Follow this path down through the woods – quite steeply for the first few yards. After approximately 200 yards, the path forks, and the walk takes the left-hand way to a recently erected kissing gate, which you go through, negotiating on the other side rocky steps which bring you down to a sealed road. Turn left along this road, which crosses the Gatcombe Brook at this point so that the brook is now on your left, and continue on, passing after about 180 yards a cave cut into the rock face on the right and, a few yards beyond, the stone-arched ruins of what appears once to have been a grotto. Ahead, and to one's left, the ruins of Berry Pomeroy

Castle rise up dramatically from the escarpment on which it was built, with the Gatcombe Brook flowing rapidly past its foot.

The walk continues on along the sealed road, passing on the right a private road up into the woods and then a group of cottages and farm buildings on the left, with a water mill visible on the far bank of the stream. Past here, the walk comes to a farmyard, where the road ends.

Ahead, two paths lead away into the fields and woods. The lower, left-hand path is private, and the walk follows the upper, right-hand path, sign-posted 'To Castle Mill Cottage'.

The walk is once again a woodland walk, climbing up through thick groups of trees towards the lodge gates of the castle, where the walk curves sharply right and west to continue along the valley side. After a quarter of a mile or so, the character of the woodland changes, to become more coniferous.

Another 400 yards or so brings the walk to a wooden gate-bar, beyond which is a sealed road. Here the walk turns left and follows the road, which for about a quarter of a mile is sunk between banks and hedges and climbs uphill, and then goes downhill again to reach the centre of Berry Pomeroy village.

At the crossroads, the walk turns left and follows the signposted road back towards the castle. A left turn between the stone gateposts of Berry Pomeroy Castle Lodge brings the walk back into the castle grounds, where the way back is downhill along the side of the valley, with views through the tall beech trees, rhododendrons, brambles and other bushes down to the valley bottom. Soon, the castle and the end of the walk, come into view.

WALK 16
PUBS
THE ROCK INN, HAYTOR VALE

(Haytor Down – Bag Tor – Lewthorn Cross – Smallcombe)

MAP:	Ordnance Survey 'Landranger' sheet 191.
DISTANCE:	About 5 miles (a shortened version, reducing the walk by $1\frac{1}{4}$ miles, is suggested).
ROUGH GUIDE TO TIME TAKEN:	$2\frac{3}{4}$ hours for the full walk.
TERRAIN:	Moorland walking with some steep sections; country lanes and roads for about a quarter of the distance.
FOOD AND DRINK:	Rock Inn; sometimes there is a hot dog van parked near Haytor Rocks.
TRANSPORT:	Car park at Rock Inn, Haytor Vale.
START AND FINISH:	Rock Inn. Grid reference: 772773.

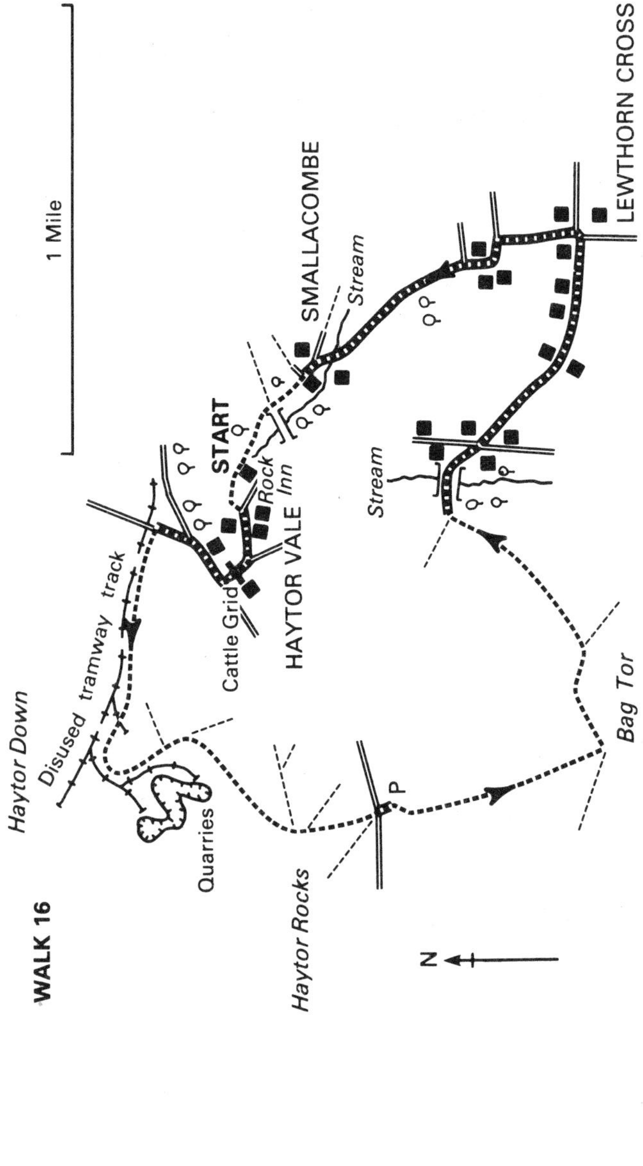
WALK 16
Haytor Down
Disused tramway track
Quarries
Haytor Rocks
N
P
Cattle Grid
HAYTOR VALE
Rock Inn
START
SMALLACOMBE
Stream
1 Mile
Stream
Bag Tor
LEWTHORN CROSS

Haytor Vale is a pleasant moorland village above Ashburton. The Rock Inn there is an old, family-run establishment offering accommodation, imaginative snacks and bar meal menus at the stylishly comfortable bar, and restaurant meals, seven days a week. It is a free house and serves real ale. Outside there is a most attractive garden for fine days.

Outside the inn, turn to the right and walk up the hill, turning right at the next junction to cross a cattlegrid and emerge on to Haytor Down. Here the walk turns right and then shortly afterwards bears left to go up the road for about 150 yards until the remains of the Haytor granite tramway can be seen crossing the road. Turn left on to the tramway and follow the course of the granite 'rails' up the moor. (Notice how the granite slabs have been shaped to guide the wheels of the horse-drawn wagons; the wheels were flat and the 'rails' were flanged, unlike modern railway practice where the rails are flat and the wheels are flanged.)

After about half a mile you come to a junction to the left. (Note the hole in the granite 'rail' where an iron blade pivoted to guide the wheels in the chosen direction.) Follow the left-hand track in a wide circle across an embankment to the foot of the now disused granite quarries which once provided the stone for many London buildings including the British Museum. Where the tramway turns right into a deep working, the walk keeps straight ahead and skirts the workings to the right, climbing steeply up through the bracken towards Haytor Rocks. The walk passes to the left of the Rocks, though you should pause to admire the extensive views in all directions. Now, you head down the moor towards the road and the car park straight ahead. Cross the road and the car park and continue along the edge of the moor, following a more or less straight line from the Rocks.

Once over the brow, the walk heads towards Bag Tor, a small pile of rocks in the middle distance, with, in front of it, a wall running from left to right with two gates close together in the middle.

When you arrive at the wall, turn left and follow it until it turns sharply to the right at the corner of the field. At this point a well-trodden path heads straight on, falling gently down the side of a shallow valley, scattered with granite scree. The walk follows this path around the edge of the moor, heading towards a row of small houses amongst trees. Soon the path joins and runs alongside a wall and trees. In the bottom corner of the open moorland is a gate and a footpath signpost. The walk turns right through the gate, and then straight ahead down a steep track into woodland.

You cross the stream at the bottom, then climb steeply up to the road.

For a quick return, you could turn left here and follow the road back into Haytor Vale village, bearing right after about 600 yards.

To continue the walk, you go straight ahead along a fairly main road which after a short distance drops away down the south-eastern edge of Dartmoor. After just over half a mile there is a cross-roads – Lewthorn Cross. The walk turns left here and follows a narrow, deep lane steeply downwards. At the foot of the small valley, it turns left through a group of houses and then, when the road turns sharply to the right, keeps straight ahead up the lane to Smallacombe. This old farmhouse and its outbuildings are reached after about a third of a mile; you pass through the farmyard, across a shallow 'ford', then turn left where the track joins another. Shortly afterwards, the track turns to the right, but you should keep straight on along a footpath which climbs up through a most picturesque wooded valley, with the little stream gurgling through the undergrowth on the left. After a while, the path crosses the stream by a wooden bridge, then a little further on, the stream passes underneath once more in a pipe. At this point, you should see on your left a short branch of the stream issuing from a cave at the foot of the sheer sides of a rocky cliff.

The path continues upwards, crosses the stream once more, and finally the gradient eases and the walk is amongst the back gardens of Haytor Vale, turning left through an old iron kissing gate, then right at the top of the path on to another path to bring you out on to the road just a few yards above the Rock Inn.

WALK 17
PUBS
THE CASTLE INN, LYDFORD

(White Lady Waterfall – Devil's Cauldron)

MAP:	Ordnance Survey 'Landranger' sheet 201.
DISTANCE:	About $3\frac{1}{4}$ miles.
ROUGH GUIDE TO TIME TAKEN:	$1\frac{3}{4}$ – 2 hours.
TERRAIN:	Clearly defined path, much of it through forest, and often steep and slippery.
FOOD AND DRINK:	Castle Inn, café in Lydford; tea hut at main NT entrance, and tea rooms at Manor Farm at waterfall entrance.
TRANSPORT:	Public car park in Lydford opposite the Castle Inn.
START AND FINISH:	Castle Inn. 510849.

WALK 17

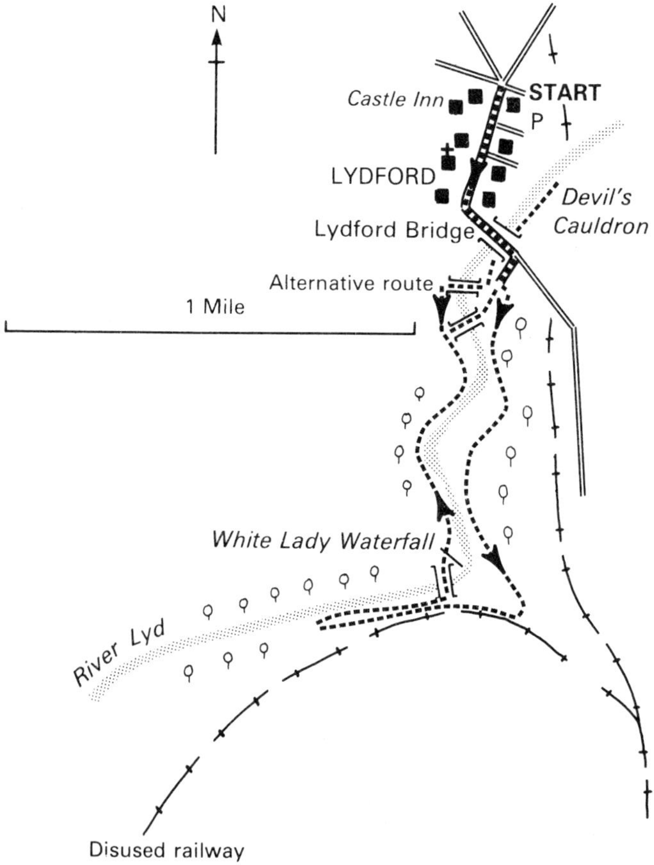
N
START
Castle Inn
P
LYDFORD
Devil's
Cauldron
Lydford Bridge
Alternative route
1 Mile
White Lady Waterfall
River Lyd
Disused railway

Lydford is a small village on the north-west edge of Dartmoor, reached via a turning off the A386 north of Tavistock. Though its greatest claim to renown comes from its nearness to the famous Lydford Gorge, it is of some interest in its own right since it dates back to Saxon times, when it had a mint, and can still show the remains of a great earth rampart thrown up as part of defences against marauding Danes. Lydford also has, in a picturesque group at the end of the main street, the fine church of St. Petrock, dating back to the 13th century, the great square keep of a castle, and a pleasant pink-painted inn, the Castle, set to the right of the keep.

The castle keep was, in fact, built as a prison for people offending against the stannary and forest laws of Dartmoor.

Lydford Gorge is National Trust property and may only be visited through the NT's two entrances and during its opening hours – 10.30 a.m. to 6 p.m. hours daily April to October (a short section from the waterfall entrance to just above the waterfall is open daily November–March).

This walk begins in Lydford, rather than at the entrance to the Lydford Gorge, so that walkers may also see the castle, the church, and the dizzying view over Lydford Bridge down into the gorge.

The Castle Inn, the starting point for the walk, dates back to Tudor times, though today it has the attractive air of Charles Dickens' 19th century about it. It offers good meal and snack menus in its two-roomed bar. There is likely to be a bright log fire lit in the bar in cold weather, while its garden is pleasant in summer.

From the Castle Inn's front door, the walk turns right to walk along the main road towards the gorge. On the right, the walk passes first the great square keep, apparently built on a mound, though archeologists say that the earth was piled up round the castle after it was built. (The castle is open at all times, entry free.)

Past the castle is the church of St. Petrock, with an

avenue of clipped yews up to it. The church, part of it 15th century, has a late 19th-century north aisle and some notable 20th-century carving and choir screen. Outside in the churchyard near the south door is an amusing epitaph on the tomb of George Routleigh, a local watchmaker.

Beyond the castle and church, the walk keeps to the main road, which curves round to the left to reach after 250 yards or so Lydford Bridge, from where one may obtain one's first glimpse of the gorge. Here, upstream of the Pixies' Glen, the gorge is a steep, deep ravine, quite gloomy with bushes, trees and plants; in this section is the appropriately named Devil's Cauldron (look downstream over the right-hand parapet of the bridge). Underneath the bridge you may see how the Lyd riverbed has been 'potholed' by boulders, brought downstream by the fast-flowing river and swirled round and round so that they gouge out holes in the Upper Devonian slates from which the gorge is formed.

Just across the bridge on the right is the main entrance to the gorge, with a large car and coach park, shop and other facilities. The National Trust recommends that visitors walk round Lydford Gorge in a clockwise direction, mainly because the paths, though well cared for with good footbridges and fencing where necessary, are narrow and often difficult, and may become crowded in summer. The Trust has available a clear leaflet map of the gorge.

Much of the walk is through woodland along or just above the Lyd; in some places, the cliff-like sides of the gorge tower above one's head, in others the lovely woods seem alive with the sound of birds. There are numerous falls and rapids in the river, including the impressive White Lady Waterfall, and a disused railway line to be crossed at its southern end. This is the section of the gorge which, the guide books tell you, is the best example of 'river capture' in Devon. It was caused by the River Lyd, which once flowed down the valley now occupied by the River Burn, cutting back from the waterfall during the Ice Age and breaking into the much steeper valley down which it now flows to the Tamar.

The clockwise walk round the gorge takes one downstream along the north-east bank of the river, turning westwards past the waterfall to take either a longer and easily-sloped path which circles through Westford Wood or a much shorter but also much steeper path which zig-zags above the waterfall. Both paths bring one down to a bridge over to the north-west bank of the river to walk upstream to the start of the Pixie Glen.

Here, the walker has the choice of either crossing the river to return to the picnic area and car park or of carrying on along the north-west bank and crossing the river further upstream to walk through the deep ravine beneath Lydford Bridge. This section of the walk has a path on one side of the river only, so the walker must return the way he came to get back to the main entrance. From here, the return to Lydford is back over Lydford Bridge and along the road into the village.

WALK 18
PUBS
THE PETER TAVY INN

(Harragrove – Merriwale – Godsworthy)

MAP:	Ordnance Survey 'Landranger' sheet 191.
DISTANCE:	About 4 miles.
ROUGH GUIDE TO TIME TAKEN:	$2\frac{1}{2}$ – 3 hours (not including stop at Peter Tavy inn mid-way through the walk).
TERRAIN:	Footpaths and bridleways reasonably well marked over open bracken and heather-covered moorland. Some quite steep hill walking, but mostly not too difficult. Short distances on sunken lanes.
FOOD AND DRINK:	Peter Tavy Inn; Merrivale Inn and Dartmoor Inn, both near Merrivale on B3357.
TRANSPORT:	In the large car park on the south side of the B3357 1 mile west of Merrivale.
START AND FINISH:	Car park (above). Grid reference: 530752.

WALK 18

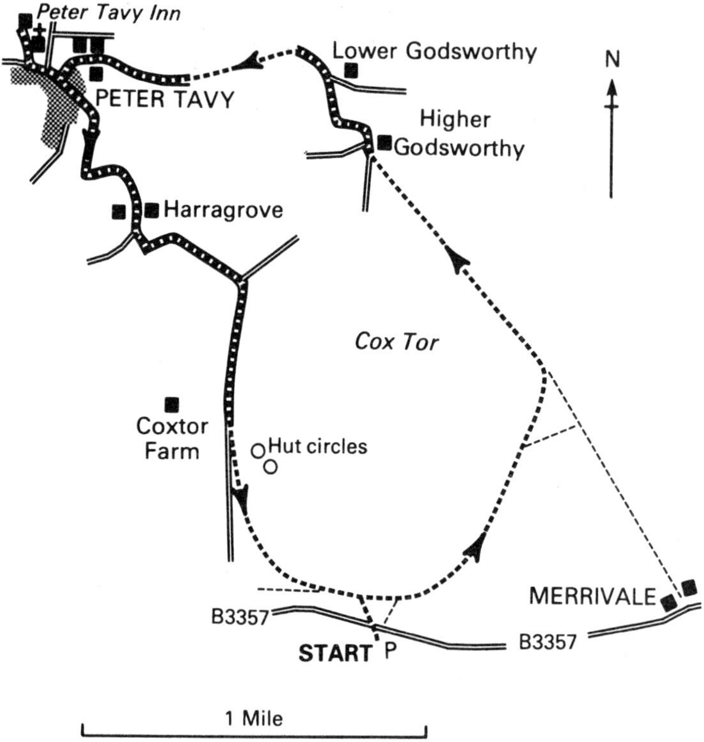

Peter Tavy Inn
PETER TAVY
Lower Godsworthy
N
Higher Godsworthy
Harragrove
Cox Tor
Coxtor Farm
Hut circles
MERRIVALE
B3357
START
P
B3357
1 Mile

Peter Tavy is a village of Saxon origin on the western edge of Dartmoor, where the moor has lost its pretty green softness of the south and become much more dour. There are great vistas of grassland with patches of bracken and heather, cropped low by sheep, ponies and wind, from which jagged tors and rocks rear up to the sky. Some of the farms in Peter Tavy parish date back to Saxon times, and the numerous hut circles, cairns and stone rows indicate Bronze Age habitation.

The four-centuries-old inn at Peter Tavy is the sort of place to which people come in droves at weekends, summer and winter, to enjoy its comfortable, welcoming atmosphere, its real ale and its good bar food. Since children are not welcomed in the bar, it really is a family place only in summer, when the kids can sit out in the garden among the fruit trees.

This circular walk has been planned to make the Peter Tavy Inn a stopping point halfway round.

From the car park, the walk crosses the B3357 to join the broad, grassy path/bridleway which can be seen crossing in front of Cox Tor, and circles round the right-hand (east) slope of the massive tor. After just over three-quarters of a mile, the path is joined by a bridleway which has come up from Merrivale between Middle and Great Staple Tors, and then bears left round Cox Tor. The farm buildings you can see below belong to Higher Godsworthy Farm, towards which the walk is now heading, reaching a sealed farm road. Here, the walk turns left, where in the field here it comes to a gate sign-posted 'Bridleway to Peter Tavy via the Combe'.

The walk goes through the gate and follows the sign-posted bridleway, with a stone wall on the right (and ignoring the path which goes off to the left just past a rocky outcrop by a stretch of ruined wall). The path now cuts across the right-hand corner of the field here, negotiating two stone walls and, with Great Combe Tor on the left and behind, crosses the Colley Brook to come to a sealed road. Here the walk turns left to enter Peter Tavy village.

The walk follows the road, turning right at the T-junction, then right again at the main village street.

A green sign with 'Inn' in white letters, points left down a no-exit road, at the end of which, past Harewood Farm, is the Peter Tavy Inn, its white-painted stone buildings set round a small courtyard.

After a break at the inn, the walk returns to the main village street, passing the church, *c.* 1500, on the left; this is worth a visit, if only to see how badly Victorian 'restorers' could treat an old church.

At the main street, the walk turns right and then left up the road marked by the pink-painted Post Office on the corner. Curving to the right, the way is now uphill on a sealed road between banks and hedges, with the left-hand bank becoming very steep after Broadoaks House is passed, though there is a view back to Peter Tavy over the right-hand bank.

The walk now comes to a gap in the bank on the left-hand side, where stone steps built into the fence bring one easily up the bank to a footpath in the field. The path skirts the edge of the field and passes through a gap in the stone wall to come out on to a narrow sealed road. The walk follows this road uphill to the ochre-coloured Harragrove Farm.

Past the farm, the walk turns left into a lane, which ends at a gate, beyond which is moorland once more. Through the gate, the walk follows the path which runs to the left of a stone wall. Where the wall turns to the right, the walk continues straight on, the path having now become quite wide and grass-covered. At the sealed farm road which the path soon reaches, the walk turns right on to the road, coming to a viewpoint offering splendid views into west Devon. A little further along the road, at a point where the walker has the buildings of Coxtor farm (still a noteworthy example of a typical yeoman's farm of the 17th century) below on his right and the highest point of Cox Tor on his left, a narrow though reasonably clearly marked path goes off from the left-hand side of the road, widening out after 180 yards or so to follow the contours of Cox Tor back down to the B3357 and the car park.

A viewing table at the western end of the car park, set up by the Royal Town Planning Institute to commemorate its 70th anniversary and to 'contribute to the enjoyment of the countryside', identifies the places, hills, tors, etc., seen on the walk down from Peter Tavey, and which extend as far as Plymouth Hoe and the sea in the south, and Brent Tor and even Brown Willy in the north-west.

WALK 19
PUBS
THE ROYAL OAK AT MEAVY

(Yannadon Down – Sheepstor)

MAP:	Ordnance Survey 'Landranger' sheets 201 and 202.
DISTANCE:	Approx 4 miles, including detour to Sheepstor.
ROUGH GUIDE TO TIME TAKEN:	2 hours.
TERRAIN:	Moderately easy hilly walk, with a short steep section.
FOOD AND DRINK:	The Royal Oak in Meavy.
TRANSPORT:	Near or just off Meavy village Green.
START AND FINISH:	The Royal Oak. Grid reference: 541672.

WALK 19

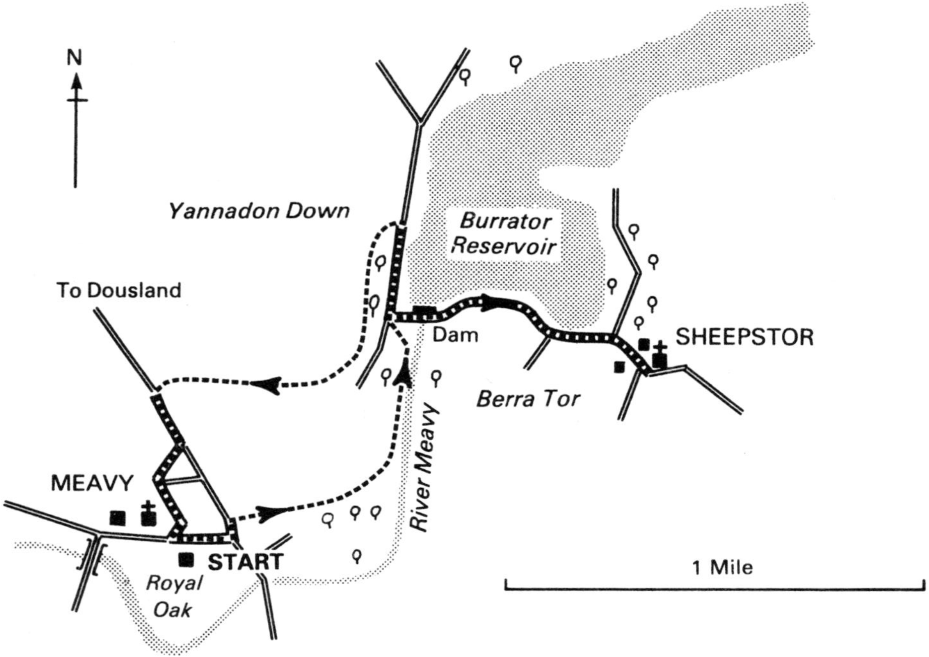
N
Yannadon Down
Burrator
Reservoir
To Dousland
Dam
SHEEPSTOR
Berra Tor
River Meavy
MEAVY
START
Royal
Oak
1 Mile

Meavy is a pleasant village with a picturesque green on the south-west approaches to Dartmoor. The Royal Oak Inn on the Green, housed in what was once the Church House for medieval St. Peter's Church, takes its name from an exceedingly ancient oak tree which grows, well propped up, near the inn's front door. Meavy's annual Oak Fair is held under and around the tree on the first Saturday in June.

The Royal Oak is a pleasant free house, offering real ales and a good selection of bar foods in its two bars and on the tables outside overlooking the Green. It is also a good starting-off point for a pleasant after-lunch walk to the attractive Burrator Gorge and the 150-acre Burrator Reservoir. The latter, created in 1898 by damming the River Meavy to supply water for Plymouth, is considered by many to be the most beautiful reservoir lake in Devon; certainly its lovely wood and moorland setting is hard to beat.

From the Royal Oak on the Green the walk goes east out of Meavy, turning left at the T-junction at the end of the village (Meavy School is on the corner) and crossing the road to go through a gateway beside a house called 'Moor View'. This brings the walk on to a path through woodland, soon crossing the old Meavy mill leat and following the River Meavy down the gorge towards the dam, whose high granite wall soon looms up through the trees. The path leads up to the road, where you turn right to cross the dam, perhaps pausing on it to take in the fine view across the reservoir to the tors beyond. Behind one, as one stands on the dam, rises the rocky height of Berra Tor (*berra* = 'wood', so the name means 'the tor in the wood'), which has given its name to the Burrator Reservoir. There is a flight of steps at the east end of the dam giving access to a steep path to the rocky top of the tor.

Sheepstor, one of the loveliest positioned west Dartmoor villages, lies about half a mile from the reservoir and is well worth detouring to, if only to find the tomb of the Brookes, White Rajahs of Sarawak, in the churchyard.

(It is also possible to walk right round the reservoir, which is about four miles round, but the walk is on a roadway, not a path, and so may not be very enjoyable in summer when traffic is heavy.)

Having returned to the dam from Sheepstor, the walk goes back across the dam and turns right to go through a wood glade edging the reservoir. From here, the walk follows the track which turns left to go uphill to what was once Burrator Halt on the old GWR Yelverton–Princeton railway (axed by Dr Beeching in 1956). The view from up here, taking in several tors, including the dramatically sheer Leather Tor to the north, and Sheepstor village, is very good.

The walk now continues along the track of the railway round the south spur of Yannadon Down. The dry channel of Sir Francis Drake's Plymouth Leat, built in 1589 to take drinking water into Plymouth, may be seen below at this point.

Where the rail track begins to curve round across the down, the path turns away to the right of it, and the walk follows the path to go downhill, crossing a cattle grid, and so coming to the Dousland–Meavy road. The walk turns left here and goes downhill for about 200 yards, where Rectory Lane goes off to the right. The walk goes down Rectory Lane, arriving back in the centre of Meavy on the village Green.

WALK 20
PUBS
THE CHICHESTER ARMS, MORTEHOE

(Woolacombe – Morte Point – Bull Point)

MAP:	Ordnance Survey 'Landranger' sheet 180.
DISTANCE:	About $4\frac{3}{4}$ miles.
ROUGH GUIDE TO TIME TAKEN:	$2\frac{3}{4}$ hours.
TERRAIN:	Moderately easy cliff-top path, some hilly pastureland walking.
FOOD AND DRINK:	Chichester Arms and several cafés in Mortehoe; numerous eating places in Woolacombe.
TRANSPORT:	Side-of-the road parking in Woolacombe on the road above Barricane Beach.
START AND FINISH:	North end of the road above Barricane Beach, Wollacombe. Grid reference: 454443.

WALK 20

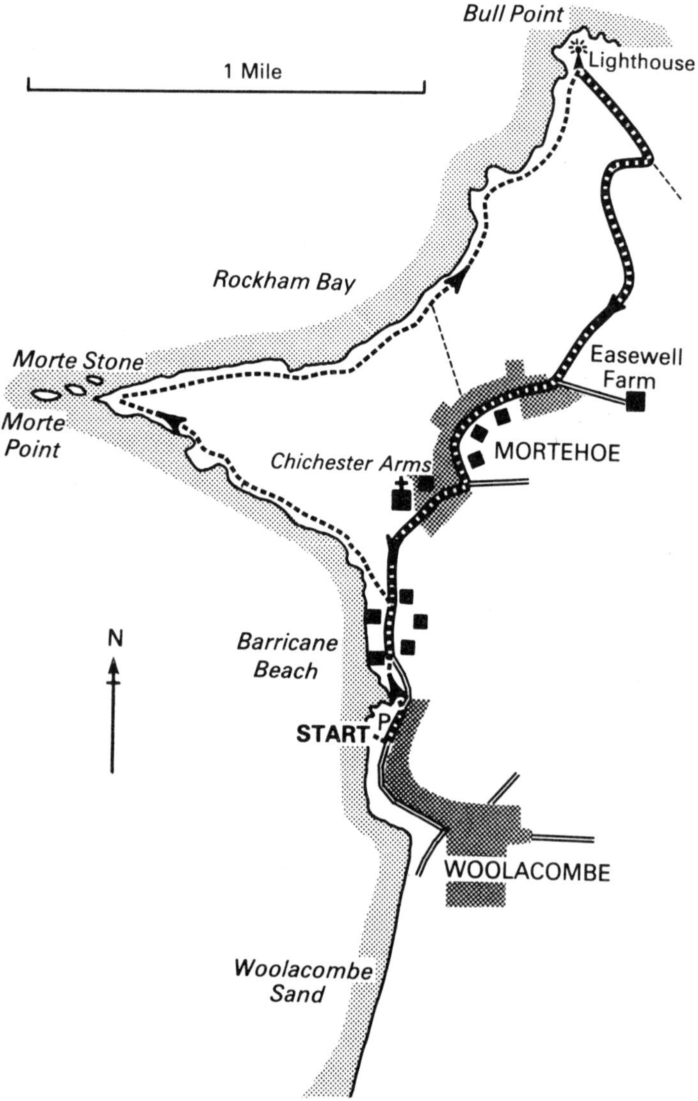
Bull Point
Lighthouse
1 Mile
Rockham Bay
Morte Stone
Morte Point
Easewell Farm
MORTEHOE
Chichester Arms
N
Barricane Beach
START
P
WOOLACOMBE
Woolacombe Sand

The Chichester Arms is a pub with a stylish air about it, not least because of the elegant white with blue facings of its paintwork. It stands in the centre of the old village of Mortehoe, on the other side of the tiny square from the interesting Norman church of St. Mary Magdalene, which seems to have been little touched since it was enlarged in about 1300. (Many people are attracted to the church by its tomb of one William de Tracey, but historians point out that this is probably the tomb of a rector who died in 1322, and not of the William de Tracey, who was one of the knights who murdered Thomas à Becket at Canterbury in 1170.)

The Chichester Arms is a good place to aim for as a rest point on a walk on the coast path round Morte Point, a particularly spectacular part of the National Trust's five miles of wonderfully beautiful coastal property between Lee and Woolacombe on the North Devon coast. Not only does the Chichester Arms have an attractive, let's-stay-for-hours bar, but it can also offer a children's room, which is an advantage for families.

From the coast road above Barricane Beach, the walk heads north (i.e. with the sea on your left) towards Mortehoe. Just where the road curves round to the right (and where the parking strip is replaced by double yellow lines) a 'coastal path' sign points off the road to the left, and the walk follows this path, which has a wooden railing fence on its left side, across greensward for a hundred yards or so (ignoring the steps down to the beach here), to come up on to the road into Mortehoe.

The familiar green and white 'coastal path' sign now directs the walk to the left along the road between the Watersmeet and Haven hotels. A hundred yards or so on uphill along the road, the coast path leaves the road from the left-hand side (note the 'public footpath' signpost) and the walk follows the coast path north-west to round Morte Point.

The coast here is dramatically rocky, given distinctive shape by the 'Morte Slates' which make up the cliffs and give it razor-sharp edges and shiny surfaces. Waves crash against more reefs of rock reaching out into the sea from the coastal path. As the path nears Morte Point itself, the infamous reef of rocks which ends in the Morte Stone (on which an incredible five ships were wrecked in the winter of 1852) comes into view off the point.

Once round the point, the path drops down to Rockham Bay, narrowing now and strewn with rocks, then rises up again to Bull Point where the lighthouse, built in 1879, now has a particularly powerful fog-horn. (The lighthouse is usually open on summer afternoons from 2 o'clock.)

From the lighthouse, the walk turns off the cliff path to follow the path/road which leads inland across the rolling green hilly pastureland towards Mortehoe. The path, a service road for the lighthouse, is easy to follow and arrives at the road into Mortehoe via a kissing gate to the left of the large gate which closes the road to the lighthouse. (There is a narrower path which forks off the main path to the left at a point where it turns sharply right after about a quarter of a mile; this smaller path leads across pastureland and allows access to some hut circles before arriving at Easewell Farm.)

The main walk, having negotiated the kissing gate (the entrance to Easewell Farm is on the left here), follows the curve of the road to the right and down into Mortehoe village. This is easy walking down a sealed road with the walls of houses and the hedges of gardens on either side.

This road ends at a T-junction (with the Kingsley Inn on the right and the Mortehoe Post Office on the left). Here, the walk turns right, along the road sign-posted 'Woolacombe'. Soon, the Chichester Arms comes into view, with the church, its churchyard entrance dominated by a lich-gate, a few yards further on down the road. From the Chichester Arms, the walk carries on along this hilly road, which is well supplied with hotels and guest houses, down to the coast and round to the road above Barricane Beach where the walk began.